Tackle and Technique for Taking Trout

TACKLE AND TECHNIQUE FOR TAKING TROUT

*How to select the right tackle
and improve your casting,
playing, and landing skills*

Dave Hughes

Illustrations by Richard Bunse

Stackpole Books

Published by
STACKPOLE BOOKS
Cameron and Kelker Streets
P.O. Box 1831
Harrisburg, PA 17105

Printed in the U.S.A.

Cover photograph by Jack Russell
Inset photograph by Jim Schollmeyer
Cover design by Tracy Patterson

Library of Congress Cataloging-in-Publication Data

Hughes, Dave.
    Tackle and technique for taking trout ; how to select the right tackle and
improve your casting, playing, and landing skills / Dave Hughes.
        p.   cm.
    Includes index.
    ISBN 0-8117-2309-7
    1. Trout fishing.   I. Title.
SH687.H763   1990
799.1'755–dc20   89-11371
                                                                        CIP

*To Richard Bunse,
who has taught me almost as much about
trout fishing as have the trout.*

Acknowledgements

I would like to give special thanks to a few people who rode to the rescue. Jim Schollmeyer took most of the casting photos and did the casting in those that he didn't take. Kerry Burkheimer, of the C. F. Burkheimer Rod Company, built a white rod blank on a moment's notice, because black rods disappear in pictures; it had an excellent, crisp action. Keith Burkhart stayed up late one night and wrapped it for me. Dick Posey, of Lamiglas, had a special glass blank built up, on the same moment's notice, for some of the casting photos, and lent an excellent graphite rod for other photos.

Photos by Jim Schollmeyer and Dave Hughes.
Illustrations by Richard Bunse.

Contents

Introduction

Fly fishing for trout has been compared to diagnostics in medicine: both are puzzles with many interlocking parts. But once the pieces are put in place the prescription writes itself, and the result is a cure in medicine, a trout jumping around at the end of your line in fishing.

Finding a willing trout and selecting the appropriate fly to fool it solve half the problems in the fly fishing puzzle. But if you lack proper tackle to suit the situation, or have the right tackle but make the wrong cast with it, you fall far short of solving the other half of the problems. And half of the solution does not entitle you to catch half of the trout. That isn't the way it works.

I got held up in a Bighorn River riffle last spring, drawing an occasional trout up to the surface to poke at an Elk Hair Caddis dry. Rick Hafele and Jim Schollmeyer had already tired of the easy riffle; they were off downstream somewhere in Rick's boat, looking for selective rising fish. I eventually ran out of riffle, jumped in my punt, and paddled after them. I found them wading a slick tailout, where a broad flat narrowed to glide into a riffle below. They both had bends in their rods. I parked the boat below them and waded up to find my own pod of fish on the flat. Solving that part of the puzzle was no problem: willing trout rose all around.

"What's hatching?" I asked Rick as I waded carefully into casting position.

"Little Olive mayflies," he answered.

"What's working?"

"Size 18 Olive Compara-dun," he said.

I found the right fly in a fly box, nipped the Elk Hair Caddis off my tippet, and replaced it with the Compara-dun. My tippet was already 5X fine, a foot and a half long, so I left it the way it was. I worked out line and placed the Compara-dun gently above the nearest rising trout. The presentation looked perfect, but the fish refused the fly. I cast again. The trout refused again. I made a few more casts to the same fish, finally put it down, and turned to the next one in the pod.

Fifteen minutes later, after putting three more trout down, I finally hooked one, played it out, and brought it to my hand. I released it and watched Jim play another trout while I dried my fly and fluffed it for the next cast. Then Rick hooked one. Most of the time the two of them had fish on at the same time.

It took me twenty minutes to hook my second fish, during which time Rick and Jim played several more doubles. I released the fish, but before I cast again I cut the 5X tippet back to a foot, added three feet of 6X, then tied the same fly to the end of the longer and finer tippet. On the first cast I had a take. I released that fish, took three more casts, and hooked another. Twenty minutes later the pod was played out, and we decided to drop downstream. In those twenty minutes, with the right tippet, I had taken five more trout.

The right fly and the most refined tackle won't help you take many trout if you don't snug the last piece of the puzzle into its proper place: the right cast.

Several years ago Richard Bunse and I fished over a western Green Drake hatch on Oregon's Fall River. It's a spring creek, flowing gently through forests of jack pine and ponderosa. Its trout are not large, but they are difficult. They rose greedily to the big naturals that day, but refused every fly we tried. Bunse is an innovative fly tyer, so we had lots of different dressings to toss at them.

Our tactics in those days were honed on rougher rivers. We fished our dry flies upstream, and took fish well from riffles and runs. But on Fall River the trout refused us until Bunse turned around, worked into position above the rising fish, and began casting downstream to them. He wobbled his rod so the line landed on the water in a serpentine series of S-curves. The line fed out on the water, the fly arrived to the fish ahead of everything else, and the trout were suddenly foolish. We took them almost at will the rest of the afternoon, until the hatch ended and the trout quit rising.

With the right cast we found that the fly pattern didn't matter so much, as long as it was reasonably close to the natural in size, form, and color. All the experimental patterns that had failed earlier were trotted out and tried again, and all of them took at least a few trout.

In *Reading the Water* (Stackpole, 1988), I discussed how to locate trout in all types of moving water, and some of the best ways to fish for them once you've found them. In *Handbook of Hatches* (Stackpole, 1987), I discussed the aquatic insects that trout eat, and how to select imitations for them that fool the fish. In this book, *Tackle and Technique*, I will discuss fly tackle selection and fly casting techniques that enable you to present the flies you've selected in a lifelike manner to the trout you've found.

I suggest you read the book all the way to its end. Then return to work with specific chapters that apply to the problems you have at hand.

Part I
Tackle

1

Trout Rods

Tackle is usually selected backwards. We wobble a rod and like it, so we buy it. Only then do we buy the lines and leaders and flies that seem peripheral to rod selection, but are truly central to it. Tackle selection should start at exactly the other end, with the fly to be fished. What a fish eats dictates the tackle that should be selected to fish for it. Tarpon eat baitfish the size of trout; you could not cast tarpon flies well with trout tackle. Trout eat insects; you would not get feathery presentations by casting trout flies with tarpon tackle.

The foods that trout eat are suggested with flies tied on hooks roughly ranging in size from tiny #22s up to large #2s. But most of what a trout sees and eats, day after day, falls in the middle of that range, sizes #10 to #16.

Food size dictates fly size, and fly size dictates leader size. The leader must be tapered to transfer the unrolling power of the line down to the fly. It must be stiff enough to lay the fly out at the end of the cast, yet light enough to allow the fly a natural drift once it is on or in the water.

The taper of the leader and the size of the fly dictate the line weight that will deliver the best presentation with the least effort. Large flies, especially weighted flies, boss a light line around; their hooks end up in your earlobes. Tiny flies fished with heavy lines go *whap!* to the water, and frighten wary trout. When everything is in balance the line loops out, the leader arcs over at the end of it, and the fly, leader, and line all land straight and lightly on the water right where you aim them. *The result of proper tackle balance is control, which is the goal of tackle selection.*

Trout tackle is in balance over a wide range of fly line sizes. Light lines of 4- and 5-weight turn over small flies at the end of fine leaders, delivering them gently. Medium lines of 6- and 7-weight turn over trout flies and leaders in the center of the size range. Heavy 8- and 9-weight lines command the largest trout flies, and the stoutest leaders.

Line size dictates reel size because the reel must hold the line, with some backing behind it. But in the fly cast the reel is not a moving part, so I'll come back to reels in their own chapter and get on to the way line size predicts the selection of a fly rod.

A fly is not a sinker or crankbait; it does not have enough weight of its own to draw line out behind it in a cast. The fly line itself contains the weight for a fly cast. The fly is just along for the ride. The power of the fly rod must be in balance with the weight of the fly line. With a line too light for it, the rod fails to flex into the curve that springs forward and accelerates the line for the cast. With a line too heavy for it, the rod flexes into a deep curve but lacks the power to spring out of it and propel the line into the cast. With the line that is just right for it, a fly rod lofts the line easily into the air, loads into a graceful curve, and springs out of it on forecast and backcast alike, generating line speed to roll out the cast, turn over the leader, and place the fly with the accuracy you need. There is harmony in the whole setup; the result of this harmony is the control you seek.

Food size dictates fly size, fly size dictates leader size, leader and fly size dictate line size, and line size dictates rod selection. Does that mean you should go out and buy all of your flies first, then your leaders, next your line and the reel that holds it, and finally get around to selecting your rod?

The rod is the living part of your fly fishing outfit. The other parts hold beauty in the way they *look*. The rod holds beauty both in the way it looks and in the way it *feels* when it moves. A lot of the pleasure of fishing for trout condenses into the rods with which you fish for them. Buying everything that attaches to the rod before you select the rod itself would be like choosing the octane of your gas before picking out a sports car.

To hell with that; get the car, then fill its tank. But don't select a fly rod without considering what kind of fishing you want to use it for. Make those other considerations first: the flies and leaders and lines that shape your choice of a rod. If you don't know the approximate purpose of the rod you want to buy before you go to a fly shop and begin waving them about, you might buy a rod that is perfectly suited to my fishing, but not suited at all to yours.

Three factors go into a fly rod to make it suit its purpose: the materials from which it is made, its action, and its length.

FLY ROD MATERIALS

There have been three ages in the history of the fine fly rod: the early age of split bamboo, the transitional years of fiberglass, and the current age of graphite. Each material has enjoyed a quantum leap in acceptance, and to a smaller degree made a quantum leap in performance, over the material that preceded it.

Bamboo

Bamboo is the material of your past and your future. Fly rods were refined to what many still consider perfection at the end of the age of bamboo. Today, nearly fifty years after fiberglass and then graphite replaced bamboo in the hands of most fly fishermen, it is still common to hear somebody say about a new graphite fly rod: "It fishes almost as sweetly as cane." If you fish long enough you'll come back to bamboo.

Before the 1850s, fly rods were made from greenheart, hickory, ash, and almost any other material that could be honed slender and straight. Natural cane, uncut, came into play during this period. It was used as tip sections for rods that had butts and midsections made of greenheart and other materials. Split cane had its first use for the same purpose: as tip sections on rods with butts made of other woods.

Calcutta cane from southern India, Thailand, and the Malay Peninsula was the first bamboo used in fly rods. The process of splitting the culm into triangular strips and gluing the strips together was refined in the period from the 1860s to the 1890s. This removed the soft inner pith of the cane, and condensed its outside power fibers, for a rod with more power for its weight. Four-strip, five-strip, eight-strip, and even twelve-strip rods were marketed before the accepted six-strip rod was settled upon. It is still considered best today.

By 1910, Tonkin cane had displaced Calcutta cane. Tonkin cane's growth is limited to a twenty-five-square-mile area in southern China. The living reed grows from infertile soils on ridges where it is lashed by monsoon winds and rain. Tonkin cane strips are powerful yet compact and light in weight. Again that goal: power to weight.

The craft of cane reached its peak during the years of the Great Depression. Then the Japanese occupation of China, World War

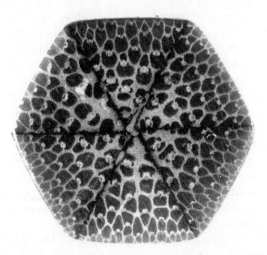

End section of six-strip cane rod. Note condensed power fibers around the outside edge. Courtesy Orvis, Inc.

II, and finally the Chinese revolution all interrupted the supply of bamboo culms. At the end of the war, fiberglass came on the market to supply the huge demand for inexpensive rods that was spurred by the sudden abundance of leisure time. Spin fishing pushed fly fishing aside for a few years, and with it went the high demand for fine cane rods.

Fiberglass dominated the fly rod market in the 1950s, '60s, and early '70s, but a few solitary craftsmen kept the secrets of bamboo rod construction alive. Shipments of Tonkin cane reappeared. With the revival of fly fishing in the 1970s and '80s, the desire to fish fine cane rods grew again. They are expensive. Demand outstrips a growing supply. But the finest bamboo rods ever made are being made today.

Because of its inherent weight, bamboo functions best in short to moderate lengths, for light to medium lines. If you are looking for a bamboo rod, I suggest you consider those in the range where bamboo works best: 7- to 8-footers for lines #4 and #5.

Fiberglass

The first fiberglass rods were built of solid glass, and had the casting dynamics of supple logs. Hollow rods came along quickly; fibers of glass cloth were formed around a steel mandrel that was then pulled out to leave thin walls around a hollow core.

Hollow glass fly rods were refined through the 1950s, '60s, and '70s. They soon outperformed bamboo at the heavy end of the trout rod spectrum, for size #7 and #8 lines. By the time graphite swept fiberglass away, glass rods were available that roughly paralleled the performance of cane in shorter lengths, for lighter lines. But not many of them possessed the indefinable feel of bamboo. Folks still bought cane if they could.

It is relatively rare to see a glass rod on a stream now. Graphite has come down in price, and people buy cheap graphite rather than expensive glass. But some of the best bargains still exist in fiberglass. Glass rods function well in the medium lengths and line weights. A glass rod from a good maker, $7\frac{1}{2}$ to $8\frac{1}{2}$ feet long for a #5 or #6 line, would give a beginner a sure but thrifty start in fly fishing.

Graphite

Graphite came in with the Space Age and swept fiberglass aside in the late 1970s and early '80s. It is a light but very strong material. Rods built of graphite are a quantum leap over both glass and bamboo in terms of the power-to-weight formula. Graphite comes as a cloth, which is cut and wound on a mandrel, like fiberglass. The result is a hollow rod that is thinner than glass, and much lighter than either glass or cane.

The development of graphite rods has gone in several directions. There are constant attempts to develop tapers that give it the feel of bamboo. If you remove the psychological factors – the life of the wood and the hands of the craftsmen who work it – some graphite rod makers have achieved the goal of duplicating the performance, and even the feel, of bamboo.

Another direction in the refinement of graphite has been toward rods for ever lighter lines. The 3-weight was conquered early; 2-weight rods have been on the market for some time and are in fairly common use. Now there's a 1-weight that is a pleasant and useful rod when conditions are right. Like most rods, it isn't very useful when conditions are wrong.

Most of the refinement of graphite has gone into improving the power-to-weight ratio. New generations of graphite appear at intervals, each one stronger than the one before it. IM6 came out in the early 1980s, and gave us rods with more punch for their weight than original graphite. Now, in the late 1980s, IMX is new on the market, and there is a marked difference in lightness and resulting line speed between IMX and IM6, which itself is lighter and quicker than original graphite.

Higher line speed is an advantage in distance casting, but it is not always an advantage in trout fishing. Greater line speed magnifies mistakes and makes them happen in a hurry. Since most casts in fishing conditions contain a litany of little errors, some of which are installed intentionally to achieve a specific purpose in the cast, most of us are better off, at least at first, with trout rods that forgive them.

The refinement of graphite has led to racks of rods that are light and sweet, that cast smoothly, and that present flies with rhythm and grace. A person setting out to select one must merely

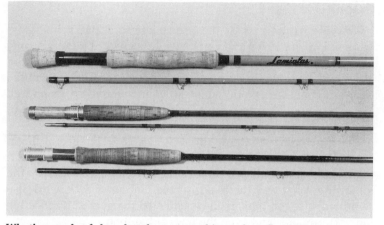

Whether made of glass, bamboo, or graphite, today's fly rod is the best that has ever been available to the fly fisherman. Dave Hughes

remember that his goal is to catch trout close at hand, not cast across the horizon.

Boron

Bamboo swept greenheart away; glass swept bamboo away; graphite swept glass away. Will boron sweep graphite away?

Boron is slightly lighter and stiffer than graphite. It is capable of attaining a higher ratio of power to weight, capable of making a slightly thinner shaft that will perform the same miracles. But boron is brittle. Techniques for dampening it to reduce breakage without hindering its performance have been worked out, but there has been no quantum leap in performance yet, or in acceptance.

Though some of the best rods on the market are built of boron, I think the age of graphite will last many more years.

FLY ROD ACTION

A fly rod's action is a description of the way it flexes when it bends into a cast. The action of a rod predicts the kind of fishing for which it will function best.

In the traditional manner of describing action, a rod is either fast, medium, or slow. A *fast-action* rod flexes most in its tip section, less in the middle of the rod, and least down toward the butt. A *medium-action* rod flexes evenly over the entire length of the shaft, with a deeper bend as it picks up load from a shorter to a longer cast. A *slow-action* rod does most of its work deep in the butt section, with much of its flex at that end of the rod, and less of it at the tip.

A new way of describing rod action makes understanding it a bit easier for me. Skip Morris is a rod builder in Portland, Oregon, and author of *The Custom Graphite Fly Rod* (Nick Lyons Books, 1989). Morris writes that rods can be described as *stiff-butted* (fast-action), *medium-butted* (medium-action), or *soft-butted* (slow-action).

A stiff-butted rod does its work toward the tip section because that is the part that loads and takes the bend. A medium-butted rod loads and bends progressively the full length of the shaft as the length of a cast gets longer and therefore the line weight against it grows heavier. A soft-butted rod loads down toward the hand grip, and bends more in the soft lower end of the shaft than it does in the stiff upper end.

Morris's way of describing rod action and the traditional way say the same thing. I think Skip's way says it better, because it describes action as a function of rod design. When action is understood in those terms, it is easier to see how it applies to fishing situations.

A fast-action, stiff-butted fly rod has always been considered best for the brisk flick-flick of dry-fly fishing. This idea is left over from the days before fly floatants that worked, when it was necessary to switch the fly back and forth several times in the air to dry it for the next cast. I began fly fishing in the days when floatant was paraffin dissolved in white gas. I can remember how Dad and I stumbled between pools, trying to keep our lines in the air as we walked, weaving tight fore- and backcasts to dry out our flies.

There are still advantages to fishing dry flies with a rod that has a slightly fast action. Today's floatants are good, but they don't float a fly forever. It often helps to give the fly a couple of flicks between floats to toss off some moisture and fluff its fibers. A rod

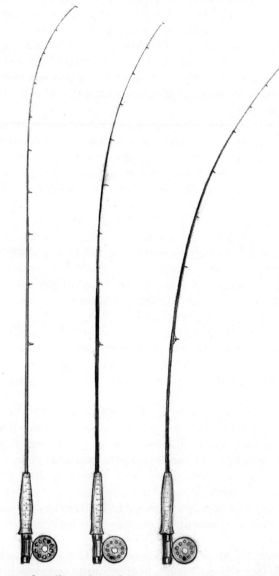

Whether you describe rods as fast, medium, and slow, or stiff-butted, medium-butted, and soft-butted, the action of a fly rod is a description of how it bends under the load of a fly line.

with an action on the fast side also offers a swifter command of the line, in the air and on the water. You can change the direction of a cast quickly, which is often necessary when fishing over rising trout or working pocket water on a small stream. You can cast tight and controlled loops, which are easier to tilt to the side, out of sight of wary fish. You can use a quick roll-cast pickup that plucks the fly vertically off the water at the end of the drift, without disturbing the surface.

A fast-action rod requires a precise casting stroke. A truly fast rod is not a good choice for a beginner; its timing will be difficult to master. A rod that is slightly fast should cause few problems.

A medium-action rod is a good choice for a beginner, or for an expert. It gives the most loop control, from tight to open, and casts most effectively over the entire fishing range, from short to long. It forgives many mistakes in the casting stroke.

A fly rod with medium action has traditionally been considered the all-around rod. It is. It fishes dry flies with reasonable quickness, or with softness when you need it. It also fishes wet flies, nymphs, and streamers very well, with a line speed that is slow enough, and loops that are open enough, so that all the moisture is not tossed out of the flies between casts.

Slow-action rods have traditionally been considered wet-fly rods, primarily because they do not fling water from the fly, causing the wet fly to float for a few feet every time it lands. Slow rods also throw open loops; in the days of two- and three-fly casts this was a help because the flies traveled in a wider arc through the air and got tangled with each other less often.

Slow rods have advantages in a couple of kinds of fishing that we do a lot of today. The first is the short cast with a nymph and split shot and strike indicator on the leader. The fly and weight and indicator are essentially the same as three wet flies. The slow rod with its open loop gives the nymph fisherman the same advantage it gave the wet-fly man years ago: fewer snarls.

A slow rod offers an advantage when fishing weighted nymphs or big streamers, especially if the water is big and the casts are long. A slow rod gives the line and leader time to straighten out on the backcast. When everything starts from straight behind you, everything will also come through straight in front of you. A fast rod, with its brisk loop, flips weighted flies around at the end of the backcast. They tangle with the line on the forecast. It is also difficult to control heavy flies with a quick casting stroke. Things move too quickly and the flies get to flinging about. *Whap!* they go on your head or shoulders.

Because of some faulty beginnings, I've always preferred rods that are a little too fast for the situations in which I use them. It has caused me some problems. My first rod was a bamboo hand-me-down missing a foot of its tip. It was brutally stiff. With a heavy line I could have gotten a bend into it, and possibly learned to cast right. But the only line I had was several sizes too light. I learned to cast by using a stroke so swift it surprised the line and whipped it into the air astonished. Sometimes it yelled *Help!* By the time I retired that shortened rod, my casting stroke was a series of jerks.

My next rod was an inheritance from an elderly uncle. It was a three-piece glass rod, $8\frac{1}{2}$ feet long. The first two times I used it, the middle section snapped under the load of a short cast. I gave up repairing it and just jammed the tip section into the ferrule of the butt section. The result was a $5\frac{1}{2}$-foot rod that would have fit without doubt into Skip Morris's classification system as stiff-butted. Only its tip quivered.

I bought a fly line that was heavy enough to tow a battleship safely to port in a storm. It was just right for that truncated rod. I spent an entire summer fishing it, took lots of trout with it, and remember the rod with affection. It disappeared while I was overseas in the Army. Using it left me with a casting stroke so abrupt that a good rod, when I finally got one, was wasted on me, and to this day I still prefer rods with fast actions.

When my brother Gene decided to take up fly fishing a couple of years ago, he invited me to his home in Montana, hired a guide, and we took a five-day float trip down the guide's secret river. Before we left on the trip, Gene asked me to help him pick out a new fly rod. We got permission to cast half the inventory of a Butte fly shop. When I was through casting rods I knew the one among the scattering of them on the lawn that I would buy for myself. But I recommended Gene buy one that was a step or two slower. He did. My own rod for the trip was typically fast.

As the trip happened, most of our fishing was from the boat, constantly casting either a big weighted nymph or a large streamer. We lofted the fly high up behind us, gave it time to carry on a conversation with a natural back there while the line and leader straightened, then lobbed it tight back to the bank. We did a lot of casting, fishing only the first few feet of each cast before lifting the fly to place it against a new bit of bank. I did fine the first day, though I had to be conscious of the timing on each cast with the fast rod, to keep from whapping myself with the fly.

By the second day of the trip, my wrist and arm wore out. I began to duck every time I punched a cast. By the third day, the guide began ducking whenever he saw my rod start forward. His boat still has chips in its paint from the constant attacks of my weighted flies.

Gene's casting, at the other end of the boat, improved as quickly as mine deteriorated. It took him a day to get the feel for casting the big flies. The slow rod responded, its patient casting rhythms worked perfectly, and by the second and third days he was able to cast more often, longer, and more accurately than I could. His wrist and arm never did get tired. As a result, he fished a particular bank while I gawked at the scenery, resting my arm, and a four-pound brown that should have been mine made the mistake of becoming his for a moment before he released it to become the river's again.

Fly rod action and length should be chosen to suit the kind of water to be fished, the kind of fishing to be done, and the personality of the caster. Dave Hughes

FLY ROD LENGTH

There has been a long-term cycle in rod length. In the days
before bamboo, fly rods were two-handed. The line was the
length of the rod, and the length of a cast was limited by the
length of the rod and the line added together. A 12-foot rod was
short; an 18-foot rod was common.

During the age of bamboo, rods got shorter and shorter as the
use of the material was perfected. Lengths passed from 12 feet
and two-handed down to 10 feet and single-handed. By the time
bamboo reached its peak, some of the finest examples of cane
construction were rods $7\frac{1}{2}$ to $8\frac{1}{2}$ feet long.

When glass came into its age, a few writers on the leading edge
of fishing advocated even shorter rods. Six-footers were used for
trout fishing on large rivers, and sometimes to kill Atlantic
salmon. But such use skirted the edge of the short rod's capabili-
ties. It took an expert to make short rods work, and the experts
would likely have acknowledged that longer rods, while less
challenging, were a lot easier to fish.

The rod-buying public resisted the trend to such short rods for
most of their fishing. By the end of the age of fiberglass, $7\frac{1}{2}$ to $8\frac{1}{2}$
feet was still the most common rod length. In both glass and
bamboo, that medium length was the most practical for the material; beyond $8\frac{1}{2}$ or 9 feet, additional weight in the rod did not
result in additional efficiency in the cast. Weight can work
against itself.

When graphite sprang on us, the material itself was so light
and strong that it opened up possibilities for rods that were
longer and at the same time more efficient. The result was a brief
courtship of much longer rods, many of them for light lines. Nine
and one-half footers became common; 10- to 11-foot rods were
offered in many catalogs.

Again, practicality restrained the cycle, and typical rod length
crept up only half a foot or so. Nine-footers are now very common on streams. It is a length that takes advantage of many
properties of graphite, a length at which graphite works well. If
the most common rod length in the best of cane and glass aver-
aged 8 to $8\frac{1}{2}$ feet, the most common length in graphite averages
$8\frac{1}{2}$ to 9 feet. I talked to a rod designer recently, and he told me

that more people are buying rods $8\frac{1}{2}$ feet long now instead of 9 feet. But the 9-footer is likely still the best-seller in graphite.

There was a time when it was believed that the longer the rod, the farther it would cast. This is true to a point, but beyond that point it is piffle. Distance casting is more closely related to the speed of the line and the tightness of the casting loop than it is to the length of the fly rod that makes the cast. When using the single-handed graphite rod, in most trout fishing situations, an $8\frac{1}{2}$-to-9-footer will cast as far as a $9\frac{1}{2}$-to-10-footer.

The length of the fly rod should relate to the purpose for which it is chosen. In small-stream fishing the obstacles to a cast are most likely to be branches overhead. Rods from 7 to $7\frac{1}{2}$ feet work well in these situations. This does not apply on meadow streams, where there are seldom branches overhead.

When fishing streams of medium size, medium to long rods work best. If there are obstacles to the cast, they are more likely to be grass and brush alongside the stream than branches hanging above it. A longer rod does a better job of lofting the line over them. Rods in lengths from 8 to 9 feet work best for fishing these kinds of waters, offering excellent control over the line both in the air and on the water.

Long rods offer advantages on large rivers. The problem is usually a twin combination of wading deep and casting long. The gravel bar behind a wading angler might be his most formidable obstacle. I don't know how many fish I have lost because I ticked my Muddler to a rock on the backcast. Big rivers also call for a lot of nymph fishing along the bottom, with short casts. The long rod lifts more line off the water, and allows the tumbling nymph a more natural drift. Rods in lengths from 9 to $9\frac{1}{2}$ feet work best for fishing big rivers.

PRACTICAL FLY ROD SELECTION

The theory of fly rod materials, action, and length will help you choose the *description* of the rod that best suits your fishing. It will not help you choose the individual rod that best suits your personality. For that you've got to cast it. In the days of split bamboo and glass, you could predict a rod's action and performance by flexing it and wobbling it on the fly shop floor. Graphite is so stiff it's different. For the average angler, it is impossible to tell how a graphite rod will cast until it is loaded with a line and cast in the fly shop parking lot.

How do you choose a specific fly rod? First, figure out what kind of conditions you will be fishing in most often – for example, dry flies on small streams, a variety of methods on medium streams, or whopping flies over big rivers. Settle on the fly line size that will carry out your mission best. Arm yourself with that line, or use the fly shop's loaners, then cast rods until you find one that whispers in your ear.

If you are not an experienced caster, take a friend along who is, one who knows how you like to fish and can interpret the shop owner's language for you. Fly shops are staffed by expert fly fishermen, which is the way it should be. But there is a tendency in shops to sell rods that are designed for experts, who like to cast sixty and seventy feet just to show that the rod will do it, not for average trout fishermen who cast average trout-fishing distances.

If you don't have an experienced friend who can get away, then patiently explain to the clerk that you are not an expert. Tell him you need his honest advice; tell him that you don't want to cast seventy feet right away, though you might be back next year to buy a rod for that specific purpose. Now here's the hard part: don't blow it the instant you pick up the rod he hands you by trying to cast seventy feet with it. See how it feels at thirty to forty feet, where most trout are caught.

THE THREE-ROD BATTERY

A hunter preparing for an African safari takes three rifles: a light, a medium, and a heavy. A fisherman preparing to purchase a new fly rod might think in the same terms. You won't want to buy three new rods, certainly not all at once. But considering rods as part of a battery can make your choice of a single rod more sensible, or it can make more sense of the ones you already own.

In *Reading the Water*, I wrote that fly rod choice for a day astream should be based on the size of the trout stream on which it will be used. The world of moving water divides itself arbitrarily into creeks, streams, and rivers. Perhaps they are best defined in terms of fly casts.

A creek is less than a fly cast wide at its widest, and can be fished in most places with short casts, forty feet or under. A stream is more than a cast across in its widest places, but the angler is able to wade into position to fish all of its water with a comfortable and controlled cast, forty to fifty feet. A river is anywhere from two to ten casts across at its widest; it has many reaches that require casts of fifty to sixty feet and longer to cover, and some that can't be covered at all without fishing from a boat.

If you choose your fly rods with these divisions in mind, you can buy the one rod that works best for the kind of water you fish most, or a battery of rods that enables you to fish anywhere, on any kind of water you encounter.

The Light Rod

The light rod has two purposes. The first is to fish small creeks. The second is to fish dry flies, wet flies, and small nymphs over selective fish feeding on insect hatches, on all types of water. For both kinds of fishing, flies range in size from #12 to #20, perhaps a bit smaller at times. Leaders vary from the length of the rod up to twelve and sometimes fourteen feet. The tippets the rod must protect run from 1- to 5-pound test. Casts are generally short, from twenty-five to forty feet. But the rod should be able to put out at least fifty feet of line when it must.

The 4-weight line is at the center of the light-line spectrum. It is an excellent choice for small streams and matching hatches. I consider the 3-weight to be a specialty line, too easily defeated by wind. The 5-weight is at the high end of the light-line spectrum, but it is the best choice for anybody who fishes often where the wind whips up on an average day.

The length of the light rod depends on which of two uses it will see most often: creek fishing or matching hatches. For tight situations, a 7-to-7$\frac{1}{2}$-foot rod works best. For matching hatches, an 8-to-8$\frac{1}{2}$-foot rod works better. If I were to recommend a single light-line rod, it would be a 7$\frac{1}{2}$-to-8$\frac{1}{2}$-foot graphite or bamboo for a #4 line.

When describing rod actions I suggested that a medium-action rod gives the most control over the widest range of casting conditions, from twenty to sixty feet. It is easy to recommend that the action of the light rod in a battery of three rods have a medium action. But most experienced casters, and I am included, prefer a light rod with an action that is on the fast side of medium. Most of us like the feeling of lightness and quickness that a faster rod gives.

The light rod should be your first purchase, your single rod, only if you fish on creeks or over hatches more often than you fish average streams with a variety of searching dry flies, wet flies, and nymphs. If your fishing tends more toward what most of us do most of the time, you should consider the medium rod as your first rod.

The Medium Rod

The medium rod is for medium-sized trout streams, which is where most fly fishermen spend most of their time. The flies cast on this type of water vary from #8 down to #18. The rod should be capable of turning over the largest of them, even when they are weighted, and should also be capable of presenting the smallest of them lightly to the water when a hatch must be matched. The leaders vary from eight to about twelve feet in length, the tippets between 3- and 6-pound test.

Again, the central question is the line weight that will handle these requirements. The line that falls in the center of the line-weight spectrum is the #6, and it will handle most flies and leaders across the wide range of trout fishing conditions. Surprisingly, there has been little argument in fly fishing literature over the years that a #6 rod is the most useful centerpiece in a closet full of fly rods, and that it is the best first rod a beginner can buy.

Obstacles overhead are seldom a factor in fishing medium-sized trout streams. Rod length should be judged with an eye toward obstacles behind, but the need for control over the line is the first criterion. Because more length gives more control, especially over the float of a dry fly or the drift of a nymph, a long rod has distinct advantages. My medium rod is an $8\frac{1}{2}$-foot graphite #6, and it is in constant use. The 9-foot length is the more popular choice, and I'll confess that for most people it's the better choice.

The medium rod must fish in all kinds of conditions, from flicking dries over riffles with tight loops that dry them out, to lobbing weighted nymphs with split shot and bobbers above. A medium-action rod spans such needs best. If you consider yourself primarily a dry-fly fisherman, perhaps a purist, then a faster rod would be better for you.

For what most of us do most of the time, an $8\frac{1}{2}$- or 9-foot rod, with a medium action and balanced to a #6 line, is a perfect first rod.

The Heavy Rod

The heavy rod is in a sense a special-purpose rod, designed to fish large freestone trout rivers with long casts and big flies, either while wading deep or drifting in a boat. The quarry is often large fish, but the casting conditions and the large flies, not the size of the fish, dictate the size of the rod. Only in rare circumstances would it be difficult to land a large trout on your light or medium rod.

Before rushing out to buy a heavy rod, recall that big rivers are most often fished in small pieces, either with dry flies or nymphs over broad but shallow riffles and runs, or with flies that match hatches on flats and tailouts. The requirements for such fishing are the same no matter the size of the water. Choose your light or medium rod depending on the situation. Reach for a heavy only if you need to cast heavy flies.

Flies that the heavy handles vary in size from #2 streamers down to #8 nymphs. Most of the time they are weighted. When the big rod is used to fish dries, which will be seldom, the flies will be great bushy things that resist the wind and tend to pile up on the leader. Leaders run from four feet long for deep flies to perhaps eight or ten feet long for dries. Tippets must be commanding, both of the flies and of big fish. They range from 4- to 10-pound test.

It takes a heavy line to turn over heavy flies. There is no displeasure in the world quite so earnest as that gained by trying to fish a size #4 Girdle Bug, its underbody wound with about twenty-five wraps of fuse wire, on a line that is too light to give it direction in the air. The minimum line weight for this work is a

7-weight, but you'll be a lot better off with an 8-weight, and you won't have to concede to a wind very often if you choose a 9-weight.

The 8-weight is the most common choice, and it falls neatly into line with my earlier recommendations: the #4 as the light, the #6 as the medium, and the #8 as the heavy. If your choices in the other categories run a single weight higher because of wind or the size of the waters you fish, then your heavy should project in the same line: the #5 as the light, the #7 as the medium, and the #9 as the heavy.

The heavy rod should be long. Because of weight, I would not recommend a heavy rod in glass or bamboo. It should be graphite. Nine feet is the minimum length; $9\frac{1}{2}$ feet gives you a bit more lift over obstacles behind you, and offers more control over the swing of your streamer or the drift of your nymph, but it is also heavier in the hand, more tiring over a long day on the water.

The heavy rod should have a slow action if you intend to lift weight with it. It is a slight problem that more and more rods for heavy lines are being built with stiffer, faster actions, based on the tournament casting stroke. They are fine for what they do, which is to cast long with light flies. But they are not necessarily the answer in trout-fishing situations.

Select a fly rod that is right for the kind of fishing that you do most of the time. Dave Hughes

A final note on fly rod selection: a versatile rod can be an asset if you fish over a wide range of conditions. But it's bound to be a compromise, and it can be a handicap if you spend most of your time at one kind of fishing, for example, matching tiny hatches on spring creek flats, or casting bushy Royal Wulffs over boisterous riffles. If you prefer one kind of trout fishing over all others, *select a fly rod that is right for the kind of fishing that you do most of the time.* Make that rod do for other kinds of fishing, or get another rod to do it. But don't make yourself unhappy by getting a rod that is slightly wrong for the fishing that you love most, and do most often.

FLY ROD CARE

Proper care of a fly rod is mostly a matter of keeping it away from slamming car doors and out from underfoot. Very few fly rods are broken on fish. The last one I broke got tweaked by a screen door when I struggled to get out of the house in the dark, my arms overloaded with waders and vests and the rod sticking out awkwardly. I inspected the shaft; there was no sign of damage, so I did not go back to get another. I was on the stream and rigged up to fish at daylight. The rod collapsed on the first cast, right where it had been pinched.

Another easy way to break a rod is to walk along with it out in front of you like a lance. If you fail to mind it, the rod will poke a tree, or droop until its tip jams into the ground. It's best to carry a rod with the tip behind you most of the time, especially if you are threading through trees and brush. If you carry it in front of you, get in the habit of holding it with the little finger of your carrying hand *over* the handle. This points the tip high, and prevents it from drooping.

The metal ferrule of a bamboo rod should be kept clean. This will help it seat correctly and come apart easily. It will also keep the ferrule from wearing and thus becoming a loose connection. The male ferrule of a glass or graphite rod should be coated lightly with paraffin or candle wax once or twice a season. This helps it seat correctly, and prevents breaks at the ferrule, which are the most common endings of graphite rods.

When joining a rod, line up the guides and seat the sections firmly, with your hands held close to the ferrule. When taking it apart, pull in a direct line, with your hands slightly away from the ferrules. If the rod is stubborn, don't pull too hard or your hands might slip and damage the snake guides. Enlist some help, but don't get into a tug-of-war, one guy on the butt section and the other on the tip. Each of you should put one hand on each side of the ferrule, then pull with increasing force until the rod comes apart, which it will with surprising ease.

Store the rod in a cloth sack with separate sleeves for each section, the sack itself tucked into a rigid rod tube. Let a rod dry before putting it away in its tube, or it will be damaged by mildew.

Most fly rod fatalities are a result of careless handling. Treat your rod, and later as you gather them your battery of rods, as if they were fragile, which they are, and they will please you for lots of years.

2

Fly Lines

Improvement in fly lines has been almost as lightning-like as improvement in fly rods, and has probably meant more in terms of advancement in trout fishing tactics. Modern plastic coatings allow fly lines to do tricks. Floating lines now float; it was an agony to keep a dry line on the surface when I first fly fished with an enameled line in the 1950s. Sinking lines now sink, some like stones. Many of the most useful modern lines do both: the forward portion sinks, the after portion floats.

Silk lines were the best you could buy in the years before World War II. They were thin and supple and sweet-casting, but they were expensive, and they required a lot of care. They had to be dried and stored in loose coils between fishing trips. They had to be dressed constantly on a trip, and even then they soaked up water before the end of a day on the stream. It was then necessary to stop fishing, sometimes in the middle of a hatch, string the line out on the grass or in the trees, and give it time to dry. Many fishermen carried two silk lines so they could pause at lunch and switch to a fresh one.

Experimental fly lines of nylon and Dacron, with various kinds of coatings, were developed just before World War II. After the war, these lines supplied the growing market because they were cheaper than silk. But they were not good lines. Their cores stretched but their coatings did not, and the differential caused the coatings to crack after short use. The cores quickly soaked up water, and the lines would no longer float. Unlike silk, once these lines soaked up water they were almost impossible to dry again.

When I started fly fishing, the first modern lines were already on the market, but the first line I got was a leftover from the transitional era between silk and the modern line. I found it in a machinist's garage, when poking about while my father talked to the owner. The line lay tangled in an open tackle box full of sinkers and swivels, dirt and dust. I bought it from the machinist for a dollar, and paid far too much. It was a level line, probably a size D, about the equivalent of today's size #5 line. It was stiff, cracked, and already ingrained with grime when I got it. I strung it on the shortened bamboo rod that probably would have been perfect with a size B line, today's size #8. I learned to cast with it; it was the line I had to startle into the air.

By the time I had practiced enough in the back yard that I felt I could approach a stream, the line coating was so shot that the line would not float for more than a half dozen casts even when freshly dressed with Mucilin. I fought it from the start of each day to the finish. That line is likely one of the reasons I developed an impatient style of fishing dry flies, letting the fly float for only a few feet before whipping it up and casting again. Five feet was a long float; more than that and the line sank so deep it tugged the fly under.

The modern fly line is a miracle. It was developed in the 1950s, when polyvinyl chloride plastic finishes were first used to coat nylon cores. The new coatings were pliable enough to stretch with their cores, therefore to cast without cracking. They were tough enough to survive the brutality of all but crack-the-whip casts. Flotation was built into the coating, in the form of air bubbles trapped during the molding process. Constant dressing was no longer needed, and drying the line was never necessary during a day astream.

The first major improvement in the modern line was the discovery that the coating itself, and not the core, could be tapered. This allowed precise control of fly line tapers for the first time, and brought about a great improvement in the casting qualities of both double taper and weight-forward lines.

The second major development was the sinking line. With control over the molding process it was possible to exclude air from the coating, and even to entrap in the coating materials that were heavier than water. The result was control of sink rate, from lines that washed just beneath the surface to lines that plummeted toward the bottom.

Three aspects of the modern fly line make it work its wonders for you. They are *line weight, line taper,* and *sink rate.*

FLY LINE WEIGHT

In the days of silk, fly lines were rated by diameter. Each diameter had a letter designation: A was coarse, B thinner, on down to E, F, and G, which were progressively finer. A typical line had a long and level thick section in the center, with tapers at each end that led to a few feet of fine, level line. A typical line designation was *HCH,* which indicated a center section with a fat C diameter, tapering at both ends to sections of thin H diameter. It was, of course, a double-taper line.

This system worked because silk registered a relatively consistent weight for a given diameter. In the early days of the modern plastic fly line the same system was used, but it didn't work for the new lines. Different manufacturers used different coating processes over the braided center cores. All HCH lines had the same tapers and diameters, but they had vastly different weights.

It is line weight, not line diameter, that loads a fly rod. In the 1960s, a new system was worked out that ignored diameter and classified fly lines by the average weight of the first thirty feet. This was a brilliant move; it allowed line selection that again made sense. The accompanying chart gives the grain weight of each standard fly line size.

Rods are designed to flex correctly, on an average cast of forty to forty-five feet, under the weight of a specific fly line. A short cast puts a lot less line weight in the air. A long cast requires the rod to carry more line weight in the air. One of the measures of a

Standard Fly Line Weight (for the first 30 feet)

#1	60 grains	#7	185 grains
#2	80 grains	#8	210 grains
#3	100 grains	#9	240 grains
#4	120 grains	#10	280 grains
#5	140 grains	#11	330 grains
#6	160 grains	#12	380 grains

good fly rod is the way it handles its rated line over the full casting range in fishing conditions.

The rated difference between a #4 and #5 line is only twenty grains. The actual difference between a thirty-foot cast and fifty-foot cast with the same line might be eighty to 100 grains. It's easy to see why it is possible to overline or underline a rod: it is merely the equivalent of changing the length of a cast five to ten feet. It's also easy to see why a person who works with short casts might want a line one size heavier for a given rod, while another person who fishes long casts might want a line one size lighter. The average fisherman will do best by selecting the line weight for which a rod is recommended. With rare exceptions, even the experts with whom I have fished follow the manufacturer's guidance. I follow it unless casting the rod tells me the manufacturer is right for somebody else but wrong for me.

Line weight is directly related to the function you want the line to perform. I pointed out earlier that fly size predicts leader and then line size. Light #4 and #5 lines fish best with flies in the range from size #12 down to #28, on leader tippets from 3X to 8X. Medium #6 and #7 lines fish best with flies from size #6 down to #16, on tippets from 1X to 5X. Heavy #8 and #9 lines fish best with large flies, from #2/0 down to #8, on tippets from 2X to 12-pound test.

Lines lighter than #4 are for specialty rods, to be used when absolutely delicate presentations are demanded, casts are shorter than forty feet, and the wind is blowing no nearer than Texas to where you are fishing. When conditions are right for them, they are excellent fishing tools, and can be a lot of fun.

Lines heavier than #9 are also for specialty situations, when the need is to launch a #2/0 or larger missile, heavily weighted, far out over the water, usually into a western wind. These flies can be miserable to cast, because of their weight, but they can also take trout that you would otherwise not be able to touch. Those trout can be big ones.

FLY LINE TAPERS

The way a line is tapered influences how it casts, how it delivers the fly to the water, how the line, and therefore the drift of the fly, is controlled once it is on the water.

Level lines have no tapers. They were once used a lot because they cost little. But they are not very useful in trout fishing because they have no reduction in size at the end to transfer the energy of the cast gracefully from the line through the leader to the fly.

Double-taper lines have level center sections that taper down to fine points at each end. The usual configuration has about seventy feet of heavy line in the center, and eight to twelve feet of taper to a two-foot thin and level tip at each end. Double-taper lines are the most popular fly lines for trout fishing, and there are good reasons for it. They deliver a fly with grace. They cast very well over the normal range of trout fishing conditions, from twenty out to fifty or sixty feet. They roll-cast well. They are easy to mend and tend when on the water, which gives the angler maximum control over the drift of the fly. They are reversible, which means you can use one end until the coating finally cracks, then turn the line around and start fresh at the other end.

Weight-forward lines have fine tapered points followed by fat bellies that taper back down quickly to fine running line. The normal configuration has a two-foot level tip, seven to ten feet of taper up to eighteen to twenty feet of heavy line, then an abrupt taper back down to approximately sixty feet of light running line. Most of their casting weight is stacked in the first thirty feet. They are excellent for casting long: the heavy front taper lets you carry a short line in the air but shoot lots of running line into the cast. They cast better into wind than double tapers. They also have the advantage of turning over heavier flies on a short cast, because they carry more weight in the forward section with

Various fly line tapers have been designed to perform various fly fishing functions. (Top to bottom: level line, double taper, weight forward, triangle taper, long belly.)

which to command the fly. They do not offer as much control after the cast, when the fly is on the water, as double-tapered lines do; the running line is too light to lift the heavy belly and move it around on the water. This only applies with casts beyond forty feet, when the light line is beyond the rod tip. On shorter casts they offer excellent control.

Long-belly lines have slightly longer fine tips, then taper in ten feet or so up to between twenty-five and thirty feet of heavy line, followed by a quick taper back down to fine running line. Their casting weight is spread over the front forty feet of line, rather than the first thirty feet of a weight-forward taper. Long-belly tapers combine some of the advantages of double tapers and weight-forward lines, shooting long casts well but still presenting flies delicately and controlling the line on the water if the cast is in the normal trout-fishing range, under fifty feet. They also have some of the disadvantages of both lines: you've got to carry more line in the air than with weight-forwards, and you have less control of the line on the water than with double tapers, if the cast is long.

Triangle-taper lines were designed by Lee Wulff. They increase in diameter evenly, over forty feet of line, from a fine point to a heavier afterportion. The line diameter then drops quickly to a fine shooting line for the rest of the line's ninety-foot length. The triangle taper has not yet been widely accepted, but within fifty feet, which covers almost all trout fishing conditions, it is an excellent line for delicate presentations, casting control, roll casting, and line control on the water. For casts beyond fifty feet, the entire triangle taper can be carried in the air, serving the same as a weight-forward taper.

Shooting tapers are thirty to forty feet long, and have the design of the front end of a weight-forward line. The tail end is attached to fine-diameter floating fly line, or to monofilament running line, with a loop. The result is a line that loads the rod quickly, develops high line speed, and shoots a lot of running line. The main advantage is distance. A second advantage is the ability to change quickly from a line of one sink rate to another without changing reel spools. The obvious disadvantage is lack of line control on the water. The light running line cannot give directions to the heavy shooting line.

A final note on line taper that is very important: the line ratings marked on rods are typically for double-taper lines and forty-to-forty-five-foot casts. When you cast a weight-forward taper, the rating is determined by the weight in the same first thirty feet of line as a double taper, but less line is carried in the air on the average cast. So it is almost always best to *use a weight-forward line that is one line size heavier than the line weight marked on the rod.* For example, if your rod is rated for a #5 line, it will probably cast best with a #5 double-taper, but a #6 weight-forward. It isn't always true; try them and see.

Many new rods are rated for two line weights, for example, #5–6, or #6–7. This is usually an indication that it fishes best with the lighter double-taper, and the heavier weight-forward. Again, you will most likely be happiest with what the rod manufacturer recommends, but it never hurts to try various lines and see which best suits your own casting style.

SINK RATES

The rate at which a line sinks dictates the depth at which you will be able to fish your fly. Since trout feed primarily in either of two zones in the water, the bottom and the top, there are lots of times when getting a fly deep is the only way to please them.

The sink rates available in modern fly lines allow you to fish from the top to the bottom in waters of various depths and different current speeds.

The *floating line* is designed for dry flies, and it is the only line that makes dry-fly fishing pleasant. A line that sinks tugs the leader, then the fly, down behind it. But a floating line also fishes well with wet flies and nymphs. It will get them just under the surface. If the water is not too deep and too fast, and the fly is weighted, a floating line will often let you fish on the bottom. Fishing a weighted nymph on a dry line, or an unweighted nymph with lead pinched on the leader above it, has many advantages over nymph fishing with a sinking line. The first advantage is control of the drift, because you can lift the line off the water and move it around to direct the fly. The second advantage is visibility: the line acts almost as a bobber. If it stops or darts, you've had a hit.

The *intermediate* line sinks very slowly. Its primary purpose is to cut through the surface film, fishing a fly just a few inches deep. It also gets the line out of any wind that might affect the drift of the fly. But you have less control of the line, because it is harder to lift a line out of the water than it is to lift a line off the surface of the water. And you also cannot see the intermediate very well in the water, making it difficult to watch the tip as an indicator of strikes. In stream fishing, a floating line will do

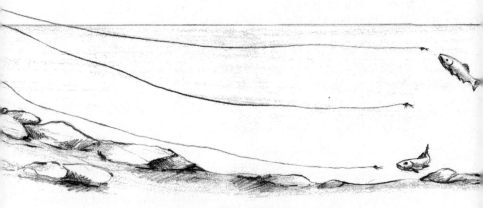

almost anything an intermediate will do. Most of the intermediate line's advantages occur in lake and saltwater fishing.

The *slow-sinking* line sinks at $1\frac{1}{2}$ to $2\frac{1}{2}$ inches per second. That's not very fast for moving water; even a moderate current takes the fly to the end of its drift before it has had much of a chance to sink. In still pools the slow-sinking line can be used to fish water down to four or five feet deep. In moving water almost any depth that can be fished with the slow sinker can also be fished with a floating line and weight on the leader or on the fly, retaining the advantages of the visible and manageable floating line. Using the floating line to fish intermediate depths also reduces the amount you must carry in your vest by one reel spool, which is not insignificant.

The *fast-sinking* line gets down at 2 to 3 inches per second, and is the most versatile of the sink rates for moving water. It keeps a swinging fly from breaking up through the surface in fast currents. It takes a fly to the bottom in two to five feet of water if the current is slow or even moderate. The fast-sinking line has the most versatile sink rate; it covers the most common situations in which you would want a sinking line. In deep water, or in runs with fast currents, you can add weight to the leader above a nymph to bomb it down.

Extra-fast-sinking lines have sink rates that vary from 3 to $6\frac{1}{2}$

inches per second. They cut through turbulence and get a fly down quickly. There are times when this is an advantage, especially when fishing big water with long casts and large flies. When fishing this way, a shooting head system works best. But extra-fast-sinking lines in weight-forward tapers are also useful for close nymphing in tumbled water. In that case the wet-tip line is best, which brings us to the need to discuss combination floating/sinking lines.

FLOATING/SINKING LINES

Lines that sink only in the forward portion, and float the rest of the way to the rod, have great advantages over lines that sink their entire length. The most obvious advantage is control; you can use the floating line to direct the drift of the sinking portion. The combination line is also easier to cast because you don't have to draw coils of sunk line up out of the water for the shoot. The full-sinking fly line has largely been replaced by the floating/sinking combination, and is rarely used in stream fishing today.

Floating/sinking lines come in three configurations: the *wet tip* sinks in the first ten feet, the *wet belly* sinks for the first twenty feet, and the *wet head* sinks for a full thirty feet ahead of the floating running line.

The 10-foot wet-tip line is available in fast- and extra-fast-sinking configurations. The fast-sinking tip gives a good combination of rapid sink rate, line control, and casting comfort. It is available in either double-taper or weight-forward lines. The extra-fast-sinking tip is available only in the weight-forward taper. With its weight up front, it bosses heavy flies well and gets them to the bottom quickly. There is often a hinge effect in the line during the cast, at the joint between the extra-fast-sinking segment and the floating line behind it. This hinge causes the entire tip to act like a heavily weighted fly, and creates casting problems on any but short casts. The problems can be cured with a slow rod and a patient casting stroke.

Twenty-foot wet-belly and 30-foot wet-head lines are available only in extra-fast sink rates and weight-forward tapers. They are excellent for fishing deeper on downstream swings in moderate to fast currents. They are also excellent for fishing deep in slow or still pools. They are harder to control on the water than wet-tip lines, because more line is under the water and the light running line of the weight-forward taper cannot command it. They have little application in upstream nymphing; there is too much line under the water to afford either control of the drift or news of a take.

FLY LINE NOMENCLATURE

We mumble about fly lines in letters and numbers. It's a code that you've got to know in order to talk like a fly fisherman, though you don't have to learn it all at once. But the code is pretty simple. L stands for level, DT for double taper, WF for weight forward, and ST for shooting taper. F stands for floating, I for intermediate, S for sinking, and F/S for floating/sinking.

The code unfolds when you add the line size. Thus a DT4F is a double-taper #4 floating line. A WF7S is a weight-forward #7 sinking line. A WF8F/S is a weight-forward #8 line that might be a wet tip, wet belly, or wet head. Its configuration will be written on its box, for example, "Extra Fast 10' Sinking Tip."

FLY LINE COLOR

Fly lines come in a lot of colors, and all of them are fine with the fish. Color choice should be based on three factors: wariness of the fish, visibility of the line to the angler, and aesthetics.

If trout are wary, they are going to be spooked by any line flashing through the air overhead. Since they peer out of a dark world into one filled with light, a white or even a bright line is probably no more visible to them than a dark line, which would be etched against the sky. The same thing holds true for a line floating on the water; a light-colored line shows up less clearly against the sky than a dark line. For floating lines the case is clear for light-colored lines because visibility is such an important factor. The better you can see your line, the better you can control its drift, and the better you can detect takes to wet flies and nymphs.

A darker line shows less in the dimness under water, especially when trout see it against the bottom. Drab colors such as brown and green are best for sinking lines, and for the sinking sections of combination lines. Visibility is not often a factor when fishing deep, but a bright color on the floating portion of the line will help you follow the drift of your fly.

I have seen little evidence, in my own fishing, that one line color spooks fish while another does not. I switched to hot orange lines on some of my rods a few years ago, because they look pretty in pictures. I noticed no decrease in the number of takes. Because these lines are so visible, aiding a beginner in both casting and controlling a drift, they are a good choice for a first line.

White and off-white or peach are the most common colors for dry lines. They serve the aesthetic sense of most fly fishing traditionalists, they are visible on the water, and they don't spook trout. They are an excellent choice, and the one that most of us make.

PRACTICAL FLY LINE SELECTION

My rule is arbitrary but simple: *use a double-taper line if you don't need more distance than it will provide; use a floating line if you can devise a way to get your fly to the depth you desire; use the line with the slowest sink rate and shortest sinking portion that will get your fly down if the dry line won't do it.*

I recommend the double-taper line because the goal of tackle selection is control. Sacrifice control only with good reason. I recommend the floating line for the same reason: with any other line you lose control. You lose another increment of control every time you select a faster sink rate, or a longer sinking portion of line. However, if a situation calls for a specific line, don't hesitate to switch. The variety of lines available today offers incredible versatility. Take advantage of it.

In the chapter on rods, I recommended that you think in terms of a light, a medium, and a heavy. Each rod serves a purpose; each purpose will be served best if the correct lines are chosen to match the rods.

Lines for the light rod should include a floater for most of your fishing, and a wet tip on a spare reel spool. I like the double-taper dry for control, and carry the double-taper wet tip, in its

10-foot fast-sinking configuration, for the same reason. These
two lines cover almost all situations you will want to fish with
your light rod.

Lines for the medium rod should start with either the double-
taper or weight-forward floater. On a spare spool, carry a weight-
forward 10-foot wet tip, fast sinking, that is one size heavy for the
rod for better casting. As an option, add a weight-forward 30-foot
wet head, in extra-fast-sinking, if you want to get down to the
bottom in big runs or deep pools. The floating and wet-tip lines
will cover most situations you will want to fish with the medium.
I would only carry the wet-head line on streams that are large,
and have lots of deep pools and runs.

Lines for the heavy should start with a weight-forward floater,
again a size heavier than the rod rating. On a spare spool, carry a
weight-forward 10-foot wet tip in extra-fast-sinking, for nymph
fishing with short casts. Another useful line for big water is the
weight-forward 30-foot wet head, also in extra-fast sinking, for
casting long with streamers and nymphs. The heavy rod is for big
rivers. When carrying it, you should be armed with lines that fish
big water from top to bottom.

**Carry the line you'll use most often on your reel, but keep a spare spool
in your vest with an extra line that covers other conditions you might
encounter.** Dave Hughes

FLY LINE CARE

There's a myth that modern fly lines thrive on abuse. It's almost true. They'll fish on and on if you never do any more than cast them. But there are things you can do to make them fish better.

It is important to keep a fly line clean. It gathers microscopic bits of dirt and debris on its coating. They keep it from floating well, or from sinking fast. They also keep it from sliding through the line guides like it should on the cast. I've heard people curse their rod after fishing a week without cleaning their line. Then they discover that the rod is as sweet as ever when the line is finally cleaned.

You can clean a fly line with a handkerchief and fresh water, but there are plenty of good paste and liquid cleaners on the market, and there's no reason not to use one. Fly floatant also works, but don't apply it to the sinking part of a line. It's a good rule to clean your line once a day, before you start fishing. If the water is dirty, clean the line whenever your casting starts to get strained. It's probably due to dirt on the line.

For storage between seasons, merely clean the line, let it dry, and store it on the reel.

Fly lines are fairly expensive. That's because good ones are complicated to manufacture. Bad ones are easy to make, cheap to buy, nightmares to cast. Save your money someplace else. Never buy a cheap fly line.

3

Leaders

The fly leader has three functions: to create an invisible connection between the line and the fly; to transfer energy from the line in the cast, turning over and straightening to deliver the fly to the water; and to allow the fly a free drift with the current, whether under the water or on the surface. A leader is constructed so that its length, taper, and tippet accomplish its three purposes.

LEADER CONSTRUCTION

Fly leaders are constructed with stiff butts, tapering midsections, and fine tippets. If the leader is too light, the cast is finished when the line straightens out: The leader towers, then collapses into a puddle, and the fly lights atop it where no fish could sort it out of the tangle. If the leader is too stout, the power of the cast punches right through to the fly and raps it to the water.

A good leader's butt section is about two-thirds the diameter of the line tip. Leader butts much stouter than that are unnecessary, and require either extra leader length or abrupt reductions in section diameters in order to accomplish the tapering to the tippet. For #4 and #5 lines, leader butts should be about 17/1000s of an inch, or .017. For #6 and #7 lines, they should be about .020; for #8 and #9 lines, butt diameter should be about .022. If you like to think in simple terms and use stiff Maxima at the back end of your leaders like I do, then for light lines the leader butt should be 20-pound test; for medium lines, 25-pound test; and for heavy lines, 30-pound test.

The midsection of the leader tapers down, in separate sections, from the diameter of the butt to the diameter of the tippet. The longer the leader, the more gradually it tapers.

The tippet of the leader is a single long and light section, its length and strength depending on the kind of fishing you are going to do. Its length might vary from eight inches long for deep fishing with a weighted nymph, to five feet long for dry-fly fishing over glass-clear currents and snotty fish. Its strength might run from 10-pound test for turning over a #2 streamer down to 2-pound test for lowering a #18 dry fly to a silky current.

Knotless tapered leaders made of nylon were used most often in the recent past. The cheap kind still found in chain stores have three strikes against them: their butts are too fine, their tapers are too steep, and their tippets are too short. They're out. Some new knotless leaders are now on the market with more thought behind them. They're excellent, especially when you fish weedy waters, because they have no knots to catch in the vegetables.

Most folks use knotted leaders today, and many tie their own. Knotted leaders work well in most trout-fishing situations, and have the added advantage of versatility. You can change the tapers and the tippet at will by adding or subtracting, lengthening or shortening sections to fit any situation.

Braided leaders are an advance in leader technology, and they work. They transfer line energy more smoothly than knotted leaders. They are supple, and give the fly a free float. They stretch, creating a shock absorber effect, protecting finer tippets. They come off the reel free of kinks. They are expensive, but one or two can last the season. They absorb water and sink, pulling a dry fly down, but this can be cured by dressing them whenever you dress your line. They transfer the power of a cast so effectively that they do not fish well with tippets of standard length. It takes a longer tippet to dampen their energy and turn over light flies gracefully. Tippets of three to five feet are standard with braided leaders. But these new leaders control the longer tippets very well, and a longer tippet is never a disadvantage when it can be kept under control.

LEADER TIPPETS

Leader tippets are rated by the mysterious X system left over from the days of gut. Silkworm gut was drawn through holes to reduce its diameter. Each time it passed through a hole it got finer and gained another X. 1X was coarse; 4X was fine, and was about the limit of gut, which lets you know how good we've got it today. Nylon leader is strong enough to be useful at 8X.

The X system is still the standard of measure when referring to fly line tippets, but it now refers to the diameter of the material in thousandths of an inch, not the number of times it has been extruded to reduce its diameter. It does not refer to a specific pound test, because the strength of a given diameter varies with every manufacturer. The accompanying chart shows the actual diameter of each tippet size, and the fly sizes with which it works best. It also gives a range of tippet tests based on some common brands. It is likely that the X system will one day disappear, and we will talk about tippets in terms of their diameter in thousandths of an inch.

The right-diameter tippet absorbs the energy of a cast, straightens, and delivers the fly at the end of the leader instead of back toward the butt of it. There is a direct relationship between the diameter of the tippet and the size of fly it casts best, which is shown in the above chart. The limits are not strict, but you will cast better when your tippet diameter and fly size fall within the range on the chart.

"X"	Diameter	Fly Size	Pound Test
0X	.011	1/0, 1, 2	$6\frac{1}{2}$–$15\frac{1}{2}$
1X	.010	4, 6, 8	$5\frac{1}{2}$–$13\frac{1}{2}$
2X	.009	6, 8, 10	$4\frac{1}{2}$–$11\frac{1}{2}$
3X	.008	10, 12, 14	4–$8\frac{1}{2}$
4X	.007	12, 14, 16	3–$6\frac{1}{2}$
5X	.006	14, 16, 18, 20	$2\frac{1}{2}$–$4\frac{1}{2}$
6X	.005	18, 20, 22, 24	$1\frac{1}{2}$–$3\frac{1}{2}$
7X	.004	20, 22, 24, 26	1–3
8X	.003	22, 24, 26, 28	$\frac{3}{4}$–$1\frac{3}{4}$

Tippet length is based on the need for a fine presentation and a drag-free float. Tippets for subsurface fishing, with wet flies and nymphs, can be short, from one to two feet. Tippets for dry flies cast over riffled water should be about two feet long to give the fly some freedom in its float. For smoother currents and fussier fish—for example, over selective fish rising on flats—the tippet must be longer, usually in the range from two to four feet, but sometimes up to five feet.

The tippet will get shortened two to three inches every time you tie on a new fly. Eventually it will get down to where you know you need to change it but you think you can get by with it until the next time you change flies. Take the time to do it; nip off the old tippet and tie on a new and longer one. If you start off with a short tippet and get refusals from rising trout, extend it. I don't know how many times I have been frustrated by selective fish, only to lengthen my tippet a foot or two, and then fool the fish with the very fly they had tipped their noses at moments before.

The length and diameter of your tippet should never be so fine that you can't turn over your fly or control your cast. It is better to get a good presentation with a heavier tippet than it is to get a lousy presentation with the finest tippet. And the wind can dictate tippet size: if it blows you've got to go stouter.

Some leader materials are stiff, some are limp. Stiff tippets can direct the drift of a fly, make it drag, turn off the fish. Limp tippets give the fly more freedom, and are better for dry-fly fishing. This becomes a factor only over picky fish on flat water, but then it is a very large factor. If you fish over rising trout, it is best to use limp tippet material. If you don't, stiff material is fine. You could carry both kinds in your vest, but I recommend you cut the weight by choosing one or the other.

You should always carry enough tippet material on the stream to rebuild the forward taper of your leader. You can carry the spare tippet spools loose if you like, but you're likely to find them in a tangle most of the time. There are many tippet dispensers on the market, and all of them work better than loose spools. Get one that holds at least four tippet sizes.

Carry the tippet sizes you use most often. For most of my fishing, that is 3X through 6X, or .009 through .005. With those I can rebuild a tippet, and the taper to it, if I need to. When I know

I will be fishing hatches of tiny insects, over selective trout, I add 7X, and sometimes 8X, to my vest.

LEADER LENGTH

The length of the leader is dictated by the amount of separation you feel necessary between the end of your line and the fly. For typical fishing with dry flies, wets, and nymphs, searching the water for fish that are not rising, leaders from eight to ten feet long work fine. They give you lots of control, even in wind. They are perfect for casting over typical riffles and runs.

For fishing fine and far off, over selective trout, the leader should be ten to fifteen feet long. The longer lengths are suitable only if they are tapered correctly and cast flawlessly. I've been approached directly by a council of brown trout, all with fins crossed and jaws jutting, and told that they do not like to winnow through a tangle of leader to take a fly.

When using sinking lines, or combination floating/sinking lines, the leader should be shortened to between three and six feet. It is not wise to get the tip of your line down, only to let a long leader buoy the fly back up. Trout do not seem to require the long separation between line and fly when feeding underwater. Some writers have experimented with leaders six inches long and fooled lots of fish.

For bottom nymphing with a dry line, your leader should be long enough to get the fly all the way down while the line tip is still at the surface. That usually means a leader between seven and ten feet long.

WEIGHT AND STRIKE INDICATORS

If you use weight on the leader, it should be placed eight inches to a foot above the fly. I sometimes use flat twist-on lead, but it requires a knot in the leader to stop it from sliding. If my tippet is longer than a foot, then the lead winds up too far from the fly. Split shot works better most of the time because you can clamp it at any point along the tippet. If you carry BB and B shot, you will be able to get your fly down to the bottom in almost any kind of water by increasing the number of shot.

Weight to get your nymph to the bottom, and a strike indicator to let you know when a fish takes it, make modern nymph fishing a deadly affair.
Dave Hughes

A strike indicator should be placed about twice the depth of the water above the weight. Indicators vary from a sprig of bright yarn to stick-on foam to styrofoam bobbers. A lot of Western fishermen use steelhead Corkies held to the leader with toothpicks. On a recent trip I was introduced to the use of thick fluorescent polypro yarn as an indicator. About three inches of it is clipped and tied to the end of the line with a granny knot. The yarn is then dressed with floatant, and its fibers flared. It stands on the water like a fan dancer's fan.

Whatever you use for an indicator, make sure it is buoyant enough to stay at or near the surface with the amount of weight you are fishing, and bright enough that you can see it on the water.

SIMPLE LEADER FORMULAS

There are almost as many leader formulas as there are fishing writers. I'll offer mine in case you'd like to tie your own. They're simple, and they seem to work. Most of the time I start the season with a leader on a line, based on what that line gets used

Leader Formulas

(These leaders are for #5, #6, and #7 lines, with .020 butts. For lighter or heavier lines, adjust the diameters up or down one or two thousandths.)

Six-foot: 24"/.020; 18"/.015; 12"/.010; 18"/.009–.007.

Eight-foot: 24"/.020; 18"/.017; 12"/.015; 10"/.012; 8"/.009; 24"/.007–.005.

Ten-foot: 24"/.020; 18"/.017; 14"/.015; 12"/.012; 8"/.010; 8"/.009; 36"/.007–.005.

Twelve-foot: 24"/.020; 24"/.017; 18"/.015; 15"/.013; 12"/.012; 9"/.010; 6"/.009; 36"/.007–.005.

for most often, and leave it there until it wears out, or needs to be changed for some dramatically different fishing. I'll rework the forward tapers almost daily, but seldom change the butt and upper midsection tapers.

I always leave a two-foot section of butt attached to my lines, again using the appropriate diameter for the line size. I use Maxima for the upper tapers, because it is stiff, and use the same material for the tippets if I am not fishing fine. When traveling to waters where I know I will be fishing over insect hatches, I carry a dispenser loaded with limp tippet material.

When I tie a leader, I leave the tippet off until I see the fishing situation. If the leader is tapered to .009, and I need one tapered to .005, I can add eight inches of .007 before tying in the long tippet, and I am ready to fish.

The formulas above include the butt sections that are normally left on the rod, and the tippets that are normally left off until I get on the water. Note that each succeeding section is slightly shorter than the one before it. That helps the leader turn over smoothly. If you want to make up a leader that doesn't fit the formulas, just work out the section lengths on the same principle, with each section shorter, and it will turn over well. If you switch from stiff to limp material, do it in the midsection, where the knots are stronger, not at the tippet, where the two kinds of materials might join with a weak knot.

4

Fly Reels

The fly reel has often been seen as merely a place to store the fly line. That is a mistake. The reel is not a moving part in the cast, but if you hook a fish that goes *whizzz!* and you are not armed with a reel that says *whirrr!* you're going to be caught saying something naughty when the fish gets away with your fly.

The fly reel should be a tool to help you fight trout. When a fish is on the run, the reel must surrender line before the tippet parts. When a fish is on its way in, perhaps sizzling toward you, the reel must allow you to take up line quickly.

The requirements placed on a fly reel rise in direct proportion to the size of the fish likely to be played on it. A small trout is often played by bringing in the line by hand, without recourse to the reel at all. A medium-sized fish, say, twelve to sixteen inches long, is usually played by hand until it makes a run that takes up the slack line and pulls directly against the reel, or until enough slack line can be reeled up to get the fish on the reel. A large fish will almost always make a run that draws out any slack and puts itself on the reel right away.

A reel should be in aesthetic balance with the rod. A reel that is too large looks like a passenger riding on a small rod. It also overweights the butt end of the rod, and makes casting unpleasant and tiring. A reel that is too small looks lost on a large rod. It can also upset the balance of the rod if it is too light for it, and can fail when playing a large fish if the spool is too small to take up line as quickly as a trout can run toward you.

Some reel types help you play trout better than others. Many are fine places to store line, but nearly useless when it comes to stopping a fish. Others are all right for tiddlers, but turn to smoke when a big trout shoulders down with the current.

FLY REEL TYPES

The *single-action* fly reel is the standard in use today. It consists of a reel housing that includes the reel foot that attaches it to the rod and a reel spool that holds the fly line and backing. A single revolution of the reel handle causes a single revolution of the

The single-action fly reel is the standard reel in use for trout fishing. With its simplicity, and its spare spools, it is the best choice you can make. Dave Hughes

spool, retrieving a length of line equal to the diameter of the spool.

The advantages of the single-action reel are its simplicity, dependability, and lightness. It also has a shape that is pleasing to the eye, in part because it is what we have come to accept as handsome on a fly rod. Most single-action reels have interchangeable spools available to hold extra lines. Don't buy one that doesn't, or you'll sacrifice all the versatility that fly line manufacturers have so diligently created for you.

Some single-action fly reels have no more than click mechanisms to restrain the spool from spinning. These are all right for limited use on very small streams, where the chance of a large fish is not just remote, but removed. Most single-actions have clicks plus spring drag mechanisms; these are perfect for most trout fishing. Single-action reels with strong disc drags might be needed where the chance of a large and hot fish is not just possible but probable; for the most part, disc drags add weight to the reel and are needed for steelhead, salmon, and saltwater fish, not for trout.

The *double-action* reel is built on the same lines as the single-action, but its gearing is such that each revolution of the reel handle twirls the spool twice around, gathering in two spool diameters of line. The advantage is obvious: you can recover line twice as fast. The main disadvantage is that record fish taken with double-action reels are not recognized, which would be a disappointment if you ever caught one. They are also substantially heavier than single-action reels. Their place is generally on rods armed for bigger fish; they are not really needed for trout.

Automatic reels are spring-loaded, and recover line at the touch of a button, which is their only advantage. You can't play fish off the reel because when a fish runs farther and farther the spring winds tighter and tighter and soon the tippet pops. Automatics are useful only for small trout that can be played without the help of the reel. They are heavy, contrary, and can snap a fragile rod tip if the button is pushed while the line is wrapped around it.

Automatics are, I must admit, disgustingly dependable. My father still uses an ancient and battered Perrine on a slender Phillipson Paramount for small, native cutthroat trout on our tiny home streams. I seem to recall that when my brothers and I played baseball, many years ago, Dad used the same reel for the ball in batting practice.

FLY REEL SIZE AND WEIGHT

The reel spool must be large enough to hold the largest line you will want to wind on it, plus a reasonable amount of backing line. When choosing a reel, make sure it will hold a double-taper line of the size you want; the double-taper takes up more space than a weight-forward line. The spool is full when the line is three-eighths of an inch from the rim. More than that and you will have problems with the line piling up on one side and jamming, or difficulty getting the spool on and off the reel housing.

The spool diameter, and therefore the reel size, is defined in part by the line and backing it must hold, but also in part by aesthetics: how it looks on the rod with which you'll use it. But the spool diameter also determines how much line is retrieved with a single revolution of the reel handle. If the spool is wide enough to be called squat, the result is a fly reel that looks like a baitcasting reel, and takes in a tiny niblet of line, about three to four inches, at each revolution of the spindle. With a fish rushing toward you, no matter how madly you reeled, you would only catch up with it after it stopped.

Most trout reels have diameters between three and four inches, depending on the line for which they are designed. These are more reasonable. Using the old formula that bored you in high school, the circumference of a reel is equal to 3.14 times its diameter. That means that a reel with a diameter of three inches will take in almost ten inches of line per revolution. It makes it a lot easier to catch up with a trout, though if the whole line is out, and you're reeling backing onto the spool, the working diameter will be a lot less, and you'll take in about half that amount of line per revolution. Still, it's substantial, and the advantages of a fly reel with a three- to four-inch diameter extend beyond aesthetics.

Backing line is braided, thin, and 20- to 30-pound test. Monofilament stretches when wound on under strain, then expands after it's on the spool. It can bend a reel out of shape. When using a #4 or #5 line, the reel should hold 50 yards of braided backing.

A #6 or #7 should hold 75 to 100 yards of backing. A #8 or #9 should hold at least 100 yards of backing, 200 yards if the reel will be used for other types of fish, such as salmon, steelhead, or bonefish.

Most reel manufacturers make their models in series, each for one or two line sizes, from light to medium to heavy, with increased spool diameters to hold the larger line and increased backing. When choosing a reel, refer to capacity charts to see which in the series holds the line and backing that you need. Your goal should be to choose the smallest reel, within reason, that is large enough for the job.

The fly reel should be as light as possible for its size. A reel that is too heavy becomes dead weight to work each time you cast. It makes a difference in a long day of fishing. A heavy reel makes a light rod feel butt-heavy, and slows the rhythm of the cast.

For light lines, #4 and #5, the reel should weigh between three and five ounces. For medium lines, #6 and #7, the reel should weigh between three-and-a-half and six ounces. For the heavy lines, #8 and #9, the reel should weigh between four and eight ounces. The guidelines are general. Reel weight is more critical with light and short rods, less critical with heavy and long rods.

Reel weight is generally a function of reel quality and cost: the more expensive the reel, the lighter it will be for the size line it holds. Many reels that fall into the proper parameters for diam-

Most modern single-action reels are made in series, with the models increasing in size to hold larger lines and more backing. Courtesy Hardy USA, Inc.

eter and weight cost less than forty dollars. The best of them, which usually means the lightest of them, cost more than one hundred dollars.

FLY REEL DRAGS

Most fly reels have a click mechanism that keeps the line from overrunning on its way out when the drag is not on. Many reels have no drag, relying only on the click to control the line. These have a place in trout fishing, but it is a narrow one. They should be used only for tiny fish, and only then if expense is a big factor. Most reels without drags are cheap.

The click on a reel with a good drag is usually incorporated as part of the drag system. In some ways a click combined with a drag is an anachronism: it's not truly needed. But the sound of the click is what we hear when a fish runs, and I couldn't possibly do without that sound. In the first place, the click makes the *whirrr* that I love to hear when a fish goes *whizzz*. In the second place, the sound of the click reports on the movements of the fish: the faster the run, the more intense the clicking, until it becomes the scream of the reel that we all long to hear. The intensity of the sound helps you determine how to play the fish. It is surprising how subtly an experienced fisherman uses the sound of his reel when playing a large trout.

A good drag is necessary to defeat a large trout, or even a small trout that knows how to take advantage of heavy currents. To be useful in trout fishing, a drag must be adjustable to protect vari-ous-sized tippets, must allow the spool to start turning without sticking to prevent reel overrun, and must be smooth to prevent the reel stutters that snap leaders on long runs.

The *spring drag* is the most common sort on reels used for trout fishing. On all but the cheapest reels it is smooth, dependable, and strong enough for the largest trout. It is adjustable. It is also the lightest type of drag, which makes it favorable for light-tackle fishing. It is adjusted on the outside of the reel, and can be quickly tightened or loosened in response to the movements of a fish, though it is usually best to adjust it once to suit the tippet, and then to leave it alone.

The spring drag has one or two *pauls* that apply the strain of the

The spring drag mechanism, with its reversible triangular pauls, of a typical single-action trout reel. Dave Hughes

drag to the reel spool. These are usually reversible, which makes it easy to change the reel from right to left hand retrieve. Most reels arrive set up to reel with the right hand for right-handed anglers. Most experienced fishermen, especially those who fight many large fish, reverse the pauls and use the reel with the handle on the left side, so they can hold the rod in the stronger hand while playing big fish.

The *disc drag* uses the same friction system as a spinning reel drag. It is stronger than a spring drag, and very smooth if it is in good working order. It takes a bit more care to be sure the discs are clean and not worn out. Its disadvantage is the weight it adds to a reel, usually a couple of ounces or more. In trout fishing, a disc drag is not usually necessary, unless one fishes exclusively for large trout. But its addition to the largest reels makes them useful for trout fishing and other types of fishing as well, increasing an outfit's versatility. Most reels with disc drags can also be reversed, for right- or left-hand retrieve.

The *rim control drag* is not really a drag as such, but an exposed spool rim that the angler can cup with his palm or feather with his finger, creating his own drag. It is generally a bonus on a reel that has a spring or disc drag. Its advantage is control – that old goal – over a fish at various stages of a fight. If the normal drag is adjusted just tight enough to prevent spool overrun, then the fish can be fought using rim control, increasing or decreasing the drag in response to the activity of the fish. A rim control drag is handy, especially when playing large trout, but the trout are rare that cause you to need one. Any reel that has a reversible drag mechanism will serve both right- and left-handed without affecting the rim control feature.

Fly reel drags should normally be set at no more than half the snapping strength of the tippet used. The line, when trailing in the water behind a fish after a long run, is a form of drag in itself, and increases strain on the leader. If the reel drag is set too tight, the added drag of the line will suddenly break you off when you think everything is functioning just the way it should. It's such an unpleasant surprise!

FLY REEL CARE

Like fly lines, modern reels function almost without attention. Almost. They should be cleaned with hot water and soap once a season, more often if exposed to sand or grit. A light application of reel grease to the few moving parts and gears completes the job. If the reel has a disc drag, examine the discs and care for them according to the maker's directions, which will vary.

Protect the reel from knocks on the stream, and store it in a padded case to defend it from dirt when not in use. Don't use it for batting practice.

5

Assembling the Outfit

To assemble a fly-fishing outfit, you need to know only four knots: the slip knot, needle knot, blood knot, and improved clinch knot. Of course there are a legion of optional knots, but these four will get you fishing, and keep you fishing for a long time. They are almost all I ever use. Two of them, the blood knot and improved clinch, you will use repeatedly while out on the streams; you should hammer them into your head until your fingers can do them almost without direction. The other two, the slip knot and needle knot, are used less often, and usually at your tackle bench.

The first decision to make, when setting up your fly-fishing outfit, is whether you want to reel with your rod hand or your line hand. Reeling with the rod hand translates into reeling with your right hand if you are right-handed, your left hand if you are left-handed. Reeling with the line hand means reeling with your off hand.

Most reels come from the factory set up for reeling right-handed, presuming that most of us are right-handed and will want to reel with our rod hands. The advantage of this: the rod hand is usually a bit less awkward than the off hand, making it easier to reel. The obvious disadvantage: the rod must be switched from the rod hand to the line hand whenever you play a fish off the reel. The hidden disadvantage: you are forced to play any large fish with your rod in the line hand, the weaker hand, while you reel with your rod hand, the stronger hand.

Most experienced fly fishermen prefer to reverse their reels so they can reel with the line hand. The disadvantage: you have to learn to reel with your off hand, which is slightly awkward at first. The advantage: you can play fish with your stronger hand, and without switching the rod from hand to hand. If you are just getting started in fly fishing, you should follow the experts' lead and your manufacturer's directions, and reverse the drag so you can reel with your off hand.

I started fishing so long ago, and in such isolation from fishing literature, that it never occurred to me to reverse my reels. When it finally did, I was awfully set in my ways. From time to time, I reverse a reel or two for a season. But whenever I pick up the reversed reel I get confused, try to reel with the wrong hand, knock fish off and curse about it. What I'm confessing here is that I reel the way I'm telling you that you shouldn't. There are rewards for it.

This summer on the Deschutes, Jim Schollmeyer picked up my rod to make a few idle casts. Everything went well until he hooked a fine fat trout. He let it make its first run, which got it onto the reel. Then Jim reached up to begin reeling in, and there was no handle there. He hollered at me and danced; my reward for reeling backward was getting to applaud an expert like Jim while he played a trout with his rod held upside down.

The second step in assembling a fly-fishing outfit, before tying any knots, is to measure the length of backing line you need behind your fly line, to fill your reel. It's simple, but it takes patience. First, reel the full fly line onto the empty spool. Tie the backing to it lightly with an overhand knot, then wind backing onto the spool until it reaches a point three-eighths of an inch from the spool rim. That's the amount you need. Cut the backing there.

Reel the backing to another reel spool, or back onto its original drum. Remove the fly line from the reel and set it aside. Now you are ready to tie the backing to the reel, wind it on, tie the line to the backing, wind the line on the reel, then tie the leader to the line, the tippet to the leader, and the fly to the tippet. When that is done, you are ready to catch a trout.

The following knots accomplish the job of assembling your outfit. You can refer to the book whenever you need to tie the slip knot or needle knot. You're not likely to have the book with you every time you need to tie a blood knot or improved clinch. Practice them until you can tie them without fumbling.

Attaching backing line to reel spool: slip knot.

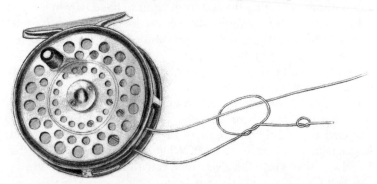

To attach backing to reel, loop backing around the reel spindle and tie an overhand knot in the backing end, around the backing line going to the spool. Tie another overhand knot in the backing tag end and draw it down tight, then draw the slip knot tight onto the reel spindle.

Attaching fly line to backing line: needle knot.

Attach the fly line to backing line with a needle knot. Begin by inserting a sewing needle ¼" into the fly line end, then out the side. Thread the backing end through the eye of the needle.

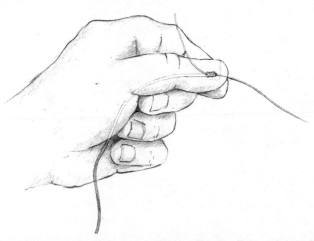

With pliers if you need them, pull the needle and backing through the line. Extend the backing 5–7 inches, and remove it from the needle.

Lay a fine tube, such as fly tying bobbin, alongside the fly line. Wrap four to six adjacent wraps of backing forward over the tube and line, then run the end of the backing through the tube.

Pinch the knot with forefinger and thumb, slide it off the tube, and draw the tag end and the running end of the backing tight to seat the knot.

Attaching leader butt to fly line: needle knot.

Attach leader butt to fly line end with a needle knot. Begin by slicing the end of the leader on a bias so it will thread through the eye of the needle. Finish the needle knot for the leader butt as outlined in the previous steps for tying backing to the fly line.

Attaching leader to leader butt, leader sections together, and tippet to leader: blood knot.

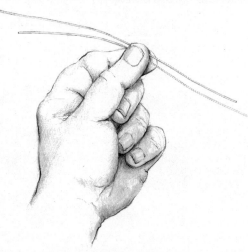

Attach leader to the leader butt, and leader sections to each other, with a blood knot. Begin by overlapping the two ends to be joined by 5-6 inches.

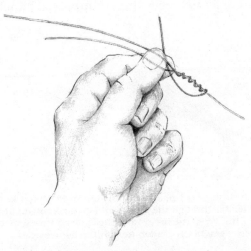

Wrap one tag end around the opposite leader section 5 times, then run the tag end through the gap between the two sections. Pull the tag through an inch or two.

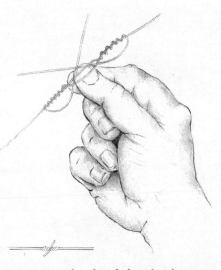

Transfer the knot to your other hand, keeping it captured under your thumb and forefinger. Wrap the other tag end around the opposite leader section, reversing the direction of the earlier wraps. Run the end through the same gap but in the opposite direction, and pull it out an inch or two. Moisten the knot with saliva, and draw it down tight. It should look like the finished knot in the drawing. Trim the tag ends close.

Attaching fly to leader tippet: improved clinch knot.

Attach the fly to leader tippet with an improved clinch knot. Begin by running the leader through the fly eye and giving yourself about 3″ of tag end to work with. Wrap the tag around the leader 5 times, then run the tag through the first gap in the leader, next to the hook eye.

Turn the tag end back through the gap between leader and tag that was formed in the last step.

Moisten the knot, draw it down tight, and trim the end close.

Attaching leader to leader: surgeon's knot.

Attach leader to leader with the surgeon's knot. Begin by overlapping leader ends 3–5 inches. Make a simple overhand, or granny, knot and pull the trailing ends through. Make a second overhand knot, pull the trailing ends through again, moisten the knot, and draw both ends down firmly to seat the knot. Clip the tag ends.

An additional knot that will serve you from time to time is the surgeon's knot. It is used to join leader sections of disparate sizes together – for example, when you find it necessary to repair the tapers of a leader on the stream, but have some leader sizes missing from your vest, and are forced to join two sizes with diameters several thousandths of an inch apart. This happens most often when you want to reduce the midsection taper dramatically, say from .010 to .006, before tying in a tippet of .005. It would be best to go from .010 to .008 and then to .006, with blood knots, but if you are missing .008, you can join .010 to .006 with the surgeon's knot.

The surgeon's knot also works when you want to attach a fine tippet to a fairly stout midsection, but don't have the reducing diameters with you. The blood knot does not hold well when tied with leaders that have big differences in their diameters.

Another use for the surgeon's knot arises when the light is low, trout are thrashing all around you, and tying a blood knot seems simply impossible. The surgeon's knot is pleasantly easy to tie. Until you've learned the blood knot so well that you can tie it without much attention, keep the surgeon's knot in reserve. It's far better to tie it quickly and get back to fishing than it is to spend the last half hour of light fumbling with a recalcitrant blood knot.

The surgeon's knot is actually about five percent stronger than the blood knot, but has the disadvantage of leaving a slight dog-leg in the leader, instead of laying it straight. This can be corrected with an improved surgeon's knot, which is tied by merely adding a third overhand knot before drawing the knot tight. But the improved surgeon's knot is slightly bulkier.

The blood knot is best if you can use it. If you can't, then use the standard surgeon's knot.

6

Gearing Up
for the Game

All the items you need to go fly fishing, in theory, are a rod, reel, line, leader, and fly. But if you're like everybody else, including me, by the time you've assembled everything you *don't* need in order to go fly fishing, you're going to need a fishing vest to carry it all to the stream. If you get yourself onto the water without some of those things that you don't need, you will be astonished at how frustrating fly fishing can be.

FISHING VESTS

Vests themselves come in three lengths and various weights. Pocket configurations vary from too few to be of use to so many that you need a computer inventory before you can find anything. If chosen carefully and stocked correctly, the fly fishing vest becomes a light and portable closet that lets you grab it and go fishing, without wondering what you've forgotten that you're going to wish you hadn't.

The right-length vest should keep your fly boxes dry at the

The properly vested angler has everything he needs on the stream, without any of it getting in the way of his fishing. Dave Hughes

deepest you wade. They come in *shorties*, which reach about to the bottom of your rib cage, *midlengths*, which hang halfway between your ribs and your belt, and *standards*, which come down to your belt line, or about the tops of your hipbones. Each of the lengths has advantages in certain situations.

The standard-length vest is fine if you do little deep wading. It is perfect if you fish in hip boots, because you can't get deep enough to get the bottom pockets of your vest wet. The standard vest is also excellent if you carry seventeen fly boxes and sixteen spare reel spools, because it has more pockets than shorter vests. But if you fish medium-sized and bigger streams, and do any normal amount of wading, you will often emerge from the water with your pockets dripping when wearing the standard vest. Then you've got to spend hours drying fly boxes and currying flies.

The midlength vest is just right for most wading, though at times you've got to hitch it up when crossing a deep run, or when working into position to fish a pool. It has ample pockets for the essentials, and cuts down the temptation to carry so much you will plummet like a stone if you topple in. The midlength vest is excellent for most fishing, and is the choice of most experienced fly fishermen.

The shorty vest is a necessity if you do lots of deep wading. It rides high, and keeps your flies dry, but has room for just a couple of large fly boxes and a few other essentials. The shorty is a specialty vest, and you should buy a midlength vest and use it until you find that your fishing calls for a short one. When you get into a situation that calls for it, you will be able to tailor your tackle to that situation, and the smaller vest will have ample room for all that you need to carry.

The material from which the vest is made can be so light it is airy, or so heavy that fishing in it is like huddling in a parka on a hot day. Some vests are now made of nylon mesh; for hot climates they are perfect. For most fishing, a vest that is made of the lightest material that is sturdy enough to stand the abuse of fly fishing is perfect. I've owned vests that were unbeatable in design, but made of such heavy cloth that they caused me to cook even on mildly warm days. You can dress for warmth under a vest, but if the vest itself is too hot there isn't much you can do to cool off.

A vest should have a combination of pocket sizes: large, medium, and small. The largest pockets should hold a single standard fly box with room to spare. The smallest should hold a couple of things the size of line-dressing tins and tiny tubes of split shot. Medium pockets should hold reel spools, leader tippet dispensers, and smaller fly boxes. Vests with nothing but large pockets are a nuisance because everything has to go into them together, and it all gets into a tangle at the bottom. Vests with nothing but small pockets are worse because the pocket flaps won't fasten over large fly boxes. Every time you bend over, the boxes dive out. It's great sport chasing fly boxes floating down swirling currents, but it can startle the trout you are trying to catch.

Good vests have at least a single large back pocket for your rain jacket and lunch. Some are zippered; some open at the sides like game pockets on a shooting vest. Fishermen who like to keep a trout or two for a streamside fry or kitchen-table breakfast can carry a small square of canvas in this pocket, to wet and wrap around the fish. Many who are surprised by the sudden desire to keep a trout find that a nest of ferns or broad leaves, plucked from along the stream, serves the same purpose.

When you try fly vests for fit, avoid any that are even remotely snug. When their pockets get to bulging, they won't fit at all. And do make sure the pockets close with Velcro. Snap closures rust, get bent out of shape, and in other ways become so stubborn you've got to drop your rod and seize them with both hands to get them open.

THE WELL-STOCKED VEST

There are certain items that should always be fastened to or tucked about your vest. You will need them often on an average day astream; without them you will not function quite as smoothly as you could.

Clippers will be in use constantly to nip tippets or clip the tag ends of knots. Fingernail clippers work fine, though the new

Some of the things you wouldn't want to be on the stream without include clippers, hemostat, hook hone, fly floatant, line cleaner, tippet dispenser, and a leader straightener. Dave Hughes

nipping tools without levers are lighter and better. There are now nippers on the market that include a diamond hook hone embedded in the back. I consider these remarkable because I like to touch up the point of my hook often while I am fishing. The clippers should be hung on a small spring retriever; you'll use them so often you won't want to dig in a pocket for them.

A *hemostat* is a necessity for releasing deeply hooked fish without harming them. It is also a convenience for debarbing hooks; make sure you get the kind that have a flat space toward the back of the jaws, for that purpose, or you will have to carry *pliers*, which means cluttering up your vest with an extra tool. I like small hemostats with straight jaws, and keep them clamped on the cloth of the inside of my vest when I am fishing, tucked in a pocket when I am not.

I consider a *hook hone* mandatory, though many people do not. Hooks get dulled on rocks and snags; dull hooks lose lots of fish, most of them on the strike. The nipper tool that has recently arrived on the market combines the two essential tools into one, and even has a needle for cleaning out the eyes of flies or picking out wind knots in the leader. It does more, and lets me carry less.

Fly floatant is available in tiny tubs or in squeeze bottles. I use floatant so frequently when dry-fly fishing that I like the type of squeeze dispenser that dangles from a key chain on the outside of my vest. If it isn't attached, I drop it often enough to make me complain. Floatant is also available as an aerosol spray; it works very well, but most of it goes up into the air or onto my fingers instead of on the fly where it belongs. I'm too thrifty to appreciate that.

Fly line cleaner is available in several forms, from a pad that clips onto your rod and cleans the line as you reel in, to bottles of dressing that you apply with a handkerchief. I managed to acquire several tins of paste dressing back in the days when a tin was supplied with each new fly line. The tin contains a circular cloth pad. Each day before I begin fishing, I cast my line out on grass, rub its length twice with the pad, then wipe off any excess dressing with a clean handkerchief. Cleaning your line starts the day off right.

I always carry a *handkerchief* in an upper pocket of my vest, usually with a corner dangling out in the wind. It can be used to squeeze the water out of a soaked dry fly before reapplying floatant, or to clean and reconstitute a dry fly after a fish has nibbled on it. It is also useful for drying your hands after you've caught a trout.

A *tippet dispenser* carries four to six sizes of spare leader material, and allows you to taper your leader or lengthen your tippet to suit the size of fly and the situation. There are lots of good dispensers on the market; all of them are better than winnowing through a vest pocket full of loose leader wheels to find the elusive one you want.

Most fishermen carry a *leader wallet*, though I change leaders so seldom while on the stream that a couple of spares in a pocket seems enough to me, and cuts down slightly on the bulk I carry. But sometimes I'm caught short of the leader I need. You might want to carry a wallet, and keep it well stocked with leaders of different lengths and tippet strengths.

An inch-square piece of rubber inner-tube material makes an excellent *leader straightener.* A leader that is kinked does not straighten out well when cast. A kinked leader also serves as a shock absorber when a fish hits, so that you feel the strike about the time it's too late to set the hook. To straighten the leader, fold the piece of rubber over it tightly, then pull the leader through the rubber once or twice. This removes reel coils, and you should always do it before you begin fishing.

Whenever I expect to encounter more than one type of fishing during a day, I carry a *spare reel spool* with an extra line, appropriate to the size of stream to be fished. Usually the line is a fast-sinking 10-foot wet tip. At times I also carry a second spare spool loaded with an extra-fast-sinking 30-foot wet head.

Strike indicators and split shot take up little room, but they increase the effectiveness of your nymph fishing by a lot more than double. They should always be tucked together into a smaller pocket of your fishing vest.

Most vests have a special pocket for *sunglasses*, and you should keep your Polaroids there. They help cut the glare, and keep you from getting headaches. They also part the water and let you spot trout, or even watch them work during a hatch.

Sunscreen comes in small bottles, and should be carried against those days when you would wind up scorched without it.

Though not everybody would classify it as an essential, I carry the remainders of a *toilet paper* roll folded flat and sealed into a zip-lock bag. I prefer it to poison oak leaves, which is often the alternative on some Western rivers I fish.

Some items are not essential to all types of fly fishing, but come in handy for certain types. They are mentioned here in case they seem like things you would want to carry in your vest.

A *stream thermometer* can tell you quite a bit about what kind of trout and insect activity to expect, as I emphasized in *Reading the Water.* A *flashlight* can be handy for threading the eye of a hook in dim light, or for lighting your way back to the car when you've been detained till dark by rising trout. It should be small; some of the best lights clip to your vest and have flexible necks so you can operate them with no hands at all. A *pocket knife* should find a place in your vest if you don't carry one elsewhere on you. My good friend Tony Robnett, who has invested several expensive Swiss Army knives in water and found that the returns are low, suggests your knife should be fixed to a lanyard. If there is a stream where *insect repellent* doesn't save an occasional day, I'd like to fish it.

If you fish often over insect hatches, a few accessories will help you capture and examine naturals, which can improve your fishing remarkably. The first rule of matching a hatch, the extensive subject of *Handbook of Hatches,* is to take a close look at the natural. An *aquarium net* lets you lift mayflies and midges and caddis from the current. A *magnifying glass* gives you a closer look at what you've caught. A small *jar lid,* white inside, is the best place to inspect nymphs and larvae, and also the best place to sort out occasional trout stomach samples. If you would like to collect insect specimens, you will need *insect vials* filled with alcohol to hold them. If you want to save adult specimens for later photo sessions, or fly tying sessions with the naturals next to the vise, a couple of compartments out of a Stak-Pak will do it; drill holes in them to give your live specimens some air.

I've listed the items you should carry all of the time, and some of the items you might want to carry most of the time. Outfitting a fly-fishing vest calls for a balance between having all that you think you might need, and being able to carry it all comfortably on the stream. If you burden yourself so thoroughly that fishing is no longer fun, then it's time to frisk your vest and jettison anything that isn't getting used frequently.

It helps, when stocking your vest, to place things in the pockets that make them most convenient to you. Items used constantly should be pinned on the vest or placed in outside pockets. Things used a few times a day should also be in outside pockets. Paraphernalia used only on occasion should be zipped into inside pockets, or left at home. Once you have conveniently arranged all of the items that you carry, then get in the habit of returning them to the same pocket every time you use them. You will soon be able to pat yourself down for nippers or tippets or hemostat without taking your eyes off the water.

ALTERNATIVES TO VESTS

There are several alternatives to the fishing vest, though none serve as such convenient storehouses for everything you might need.

The first alternative is the old creel. Wicker creels were fine for their main purpose, which was keeping dead trout fresh. But killing trout is now an activity out on the periphery of trout fishing; the wicker creel, with all its vast bulk and weight, is seldom seen. The canvas creel, lying flat against your side, is less of a nuisance. But it is essentially one big pocket, perhaps two. Everything gets stirred together inside; every time you need something you've got to rummage around for it.

A new alternative to the old creel is a boxlike nylon bag that hangs at your side like a wicker creel, but is smaller and more convenient and has many divisions to separate the gadgetry that is necessary to fly fishing. These bags are excellent, especially in their smaller sizes; they carry everything you need but are not a garment like a vest. They let you travel light and cool. In the larger sizes they are perfect for carrying peripheral gear, as backup bags to your vest, kept in the car or the boat. They hold things like extra reels and spare spools and leader-tying kits that you don't always want on your person on a trip, but don't want far from you, and don't want to hunt for when you need them. I use one of these bags whenever I float a river, in addition to my vest. I leave it in the boat when I get out to wade and fish, but refer to it often for lunch, film for the camera, a new leader, or a reel for the big rod that I use to punch flies to the banks between gravel bar stops. I also leave many special-purpose fly boxes in it, the kind that I might need, but don't want to burden myself with until I do need them.

Another alternative to the vest is the chest fly box. Various versions carry inventories of flies and small batteries of tools. Most have the disadvantage of lacking pockets, making it difficult to tailor your equipage to your own needs. Some have the advantage of interchangeable fly drawers, which lets you shuttle your inventory as the season progresses, and as hatch succeeds hatch. A minor disadvantage: chest boxes harness to you, and do not allow you to carry either camera or binoculars on the traditional neck strap.

There are several new products on the market that I call *minimum bags*. They come in various configurations, but their size is tiny, and they attach to your belt, hang over your shoulder like a purse, or dangle around your neck like a light camera. They hold a fly box or two, have a few tiny pockets for tippets and tools, plus attachments for clippers and floatant. They don't cost much. They are a release on those days when you want to travel light, far up a stream, and know that a few fly patterns will get you enough trout to make you happy. If you select your flies carefully,

Alternatives to the fishing vest include (from left) the Wood River Bag, chest boxes such as the Hatch System, and minimum bags such as the Sidekick II. Dave Hughes

minimum bags will serve in a surprisingly wide variety of trout stream situations.

The fishing shirt is an alternative to the fishing vest. All of the major fishing catalogs offer a shirt with four large front pockets and a lunch pocket in the back. In good weather, on a stream where you know what you will encounter, and therefore what you will need for a day of fishing, you can carry everything you need in the pockets of the shirt. It lets you go light. I normally use only a fishing shirt when fishing my tiny home creeks. An untucked cotton shirt, with a few items squirreled in its pockets, is perfect transportation for exploring down a desert stream in the summer sun.

FLY BOXES

Fly boxes come in a wider variety than there is room to write about here. The basic types, however, hold either dry flies or wet flies, nymphs, and streamers. The difference is elemental: dry flies have bristling hackles, and need lots of room or the hackles get matted down; sunk flies have swept-back hackles, and it doesn't matter if they get slightly cramped.

Dry-fly boxes have compartments with dividers between them. The simplest and possibly the best of them are made of shatterproof plastic with transparent lids so you can see the flies through them. They come in various sizes, and are divided into a variety of compartments. The size to choose for your main fly boxes are those that fit into the pockets of your vest conveniently, and are divided so that they hold half a dozen or more of your favorite flies in each compartment without mashing the hackles. If I were to name a standard size, it would be about six inches long by three inches wide and an inch deep. It would have eight compartments of equal size.

I recommend starting with a couple of these, one filled with traditional dries like the Adams and Light and Dark Cahills in a narrow range of sizes. The other should hold searching dressings such as the Elk Hair Caddis, Royal Wulff, and Humpy, again in a narrow range of sizes. *Handbook of Hatches* suggests more comprehensive ways to select your flies, and to put them in order.

You can use compartmented fly boxes for wet flies, nymphs,

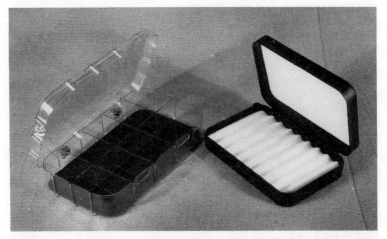

Partitioned boxes are best for dry flies; ripple foam boxes keep wets, nymphs, and streamers in better shape, and more organized. Dave Hughes

and streamers. But boxes that hold them rigidly in rows show them off better, and let you choose more carefully from among them. Newer plastic boxes have inserts of ridged foam. There is little doubt that these hold the most wets and nymphs with the most convenience, and do the least to muss up their wings and legs and hackles and whatever other parts they possess. These boxes even work well for dry flies.

One wet-fly-and-nymph box will get you started. Fill it with a small selection of standard wets like the Cahills, Hare's Ear, and Alder to cover the range of natural insect colors. Add effective searching nymphs such as the Zug Bug, Gold Ribbed Hare's Ear, and Muskrat, again in a range of sizes. A few small Muddlers and Woolly Bugger streamers should fill it up. Add another box and increase your selection as you encounter situations that demand specific dressings.

I use one additional kind of fly box: the minibox. Some of these I buy, for their tiny compartments, which hold tiny midge and mayfly dries. Others I make myself, by glueing styrofoam into cough-drop tins and even tiny aspirin tins. These hold midge pupal patterns, small Pheasant Tails, and other nymphs that match specific insects.

WADERS AND ACCESSORIES

Like rods and reels and vests, waders should suit the kind of fishing that you do most often. There are a couple of basic kinds of waders.

Boot-foot waders have the feet attached to the legs, built in as part of the waders. The waders are usually rubber, and they tend to be bulky and awkward and not quite tight-fitting on the feet, so they aren't the best for long days that include heavy hiking. Ten years ago, boot-foot waders were almost all you saw. Today they have been replaced by stocking-foot waders, and you seldom see a pair of boot-foots. But they are marvelously convenient when you fish from place to place, getting in and out of your car for an hour here and two hours there. You can slip into them and back out quickly, and don't tend to put them on and stay in them all day as you do stocking-foot waders.

Stocking-foot waders have waterproof feet but no attached boots. Wading shoes lace over them. The result is a more convenient package when they are rolled and carried or stored, and better protection for your feet when you are fishing. They also allow a certain versatility if you own more than one kind of wading shoe. You can change from one to the other to suit the water and bottom type.

Stocking-foot waders are made from a variety of materials. The lightest are made of rubberized nylon; they roll into a small package for travel, and they are flexible and comfortable when you are fishing. If you want to cover much ground during a day's fishing, they are the best way to go. But they are thin; if the water is cold, it is hard to wear enough layers under them to keep your legs warm. For normal trout-fishing temperatures, they are excellent.

Neoprene waders are thick, made from wetsuit material, and cannot be matched for warmth. They are by far the most popular now; they are almost a mandatory part of the fly fisher's uniform. There is little question of their warmth and comfort, both in and out of the water. If you must spend a day sitting in a boat in windy and wet weather, they are also the perfect rain gear. They are flexible and they stretch, allowing you to climb over the gunwale of a drift boat with a bit of agility not available in most waders. Their material is buoyant; if you fall in you've got a built-in life preserver.

Neoprene waders are expensive, but they earn their way, and deserve their popularity. They have one drawback: because they are buoyant they tend to float you a bit as you wade. This is fine in normal situations, but when you wade deep in pushy currents, it can be a problem.

I fished the Deschutes River for summer steelhead once with Frank Amato. Its steelhead water is broad and deep and strong. I noticed that as Frank followed me through a run, he waded almost twenty feet farther out, and covered more water than I did. That's an advantage when fishing for summer steelhead. I tried to edge out, but immediately had trouble keeping my feet on the bottom. I seemed to be about to float away. Frank is about my size, and I couldn't figure out why he was comfortable in water that put me in danger.

That afternoon we talked about it, and Frank lent me a pair of nylon waders to try in place of my neoprenes. The difference was surprising; I had no trouble wading the deeper and stronger water, though I had to wear an extra pair of pile pants under the waders to keep warm.

I own nearly a closetful of waders now. I wear neoprenes in spring and fall, nylons in summer. If the river is strong, I stick

The right waders let you wade deep, fish comfortably, and stay warm all day. Dave Hughes

with nylon waders even if the water is cold. I'd rather my discomfort be cold legs than a lack of control when I'm wading.

Hip boots are not waders, but they are comfortable when you aren't wading deep enough to need waders. I rarely use them on fishing trips because I never know when I will want to wade deep to reach an enticing bit of water, even on small- to medium-sized streams. But hippers with felt soles are perfect for tiny creeks, where you seldom go in above your knees.

Care of waders is simple. Dry them out between trips, and store them where the sun can't strike them. Keep them away from oil and gas and sharp things. Wader repair varies with the material from which they are made. When you buy a new pair, also buy a repair kit, and keep it in your backup bag. Vinyl repair tape will make a quick emergency repair in most waders. Shoe Goo or Goop will plug up holes, and dry quickly enough to get you back to fishing fast. Permanent repairs can often wait until you get home.

WADING SHOES

Wading shoes are made of nylon or of synthetic leathers. The first are light, and perfect for air travel or long days spent hiking. The latter are heavier, and give better protection to your feet. That becomes an important factor when you spend lots of time wading; your feet battle rocks on the bottom all day, and by the end of the day can be battered unless you wear sturdy wading shoes.

What you have on the bottoms of your wading shoes makes far more difference than the material from which they are built. Leather, rubber, or synthetic soles are a little like grease on smooth wet stones. If I had only ten dollars to spend on fly fishing tackle, I'd spend it on carpet or felt, glue it to old tennis shoes, and fish with a willow switch before I'd spend it on some fancy bit of gear. Fly fishing is not fun if you can't do it standing up.

Felt soles work best on clean stream bottoms, and should be the first choice for all but a few fishermen. Felt does not get the best grip on rocks that are slick with algae. Sandals can be bought that fit over your felted wading shoes, with soles armed with aluminum cleats or tire studs. Aluminum gets the best grip, but wears down quickly. Steel studs can make you prance on bare rock, and they pop out more often than you'd like. But they can be replaced, and they don't wear down. So far I haven't found the best thing to wear on slick bottoms, so I still use felt and a staff and wade with lots of care when I get onto rocks coated with algae.

When you buy wading shoes, make sure you try them on with your waders on, and wear the same thick socks you will wear when fishing. Put a final pair of wool socks on the *outside* of the waders to protect them from chafing by the boots and by gravel that gathers in the boots. You can also buy gravel guards that zip over the tops of the boots, eliminating the need for that last pair of socks.

WADING ACCESSORIES

A *wading belt* snugs around your middle, outside your waders, and seals you in. If you take a spill, your waders don't fill with water. You won't drown even if they do—water tends to have a neutral buoyancy in water so it doesn't pull you down—but you will get wet all the way down to your toes, and you'll think you *are* the river when you get to shore and try to climb out of it.

A *wading staff* is a third leg, and turns you into a tripod in heavy currents. I hate to carry one all the time because it is constantly in the way; I also hate to be without one. I now have one that folds into foot-long sections, rests out of the way in a holster on my wading belt, but springs and locks straight when I draw it. I seldom fish without it. A cord about three feet long serves to attach the staff to my wading belt.

CLOTHING FOR FISHING

Advice on clothing will be brief, based on the assumption that you already know how to dress yourself. But there are a few things that my fishing partners have taught me, and I'd like you to know them, too.

Denims and khakis and most of what we normally wear for pants bind when you wear them under waders. It's tempting to just pull your waders over what you are already wearing, but try pulling them over long-john bottoms instead, or joggers' sweat pants. You will be surprised at the freedom of movement it gives you. If the water and the weather are warm, pull your waders over shorts. If the water is cold, wear thick-pile pants. Don't wear goose down: it gets its warmth from loft; water pressure collapses it, and down quickly becomes the next thing to wearing nothing.

There isn't much to say about fishing shirts except that they should be roomy, long enough to tuck in, and long-sleeved if mosquitoes and the sun are around. I have a grievance against shirt manufacturers who design fashionable but dainty pockets with flaps that won't button over a fly box, or a small notebook and pen, but I think it could be called a personal problem unless I find out that lots of you are mad about it, too. If the weather is cold, your shirt should be warm; if the weather is hot, your shirt should be cool. Maybe it's time to go on to the next subject.

The best rainpants are your waders. A good slicker is light in weight, just long enough to cover your vest, and large enough to fit over your vest when the vest is stuffed with fly boxes. The slicker hood should be designed to fit over a hat, not under it. The slicker should have deep pockets. Some new slickers are designed especially for fishing: they have slices for pockets but not their bottoms, so you can reach through and filch things out of your vest without taking the slicker off.

Fishing hats should protect your neck and ears from sunburn. The brim should extend far enough to shade your eyes; without shade it is very difficult to see into water, even with Polaroids. The hat should be waterproof if the climate is likely to surprise you, which most climates are. If the weather gets windy, a chin strap will keep the hat on your head.

Fingerless wool or neoprene gloves are surprisingly warm, and will keep you on the water a few extra hours on some bitter days. They also allow you the dexterity you would not have if you had no gloves, and your hands got numb. Like other items that you might need only at times, you won't always want to carry your gloves, but you should have them where you can reach them if the weather threatens to bluster.

Landing nets are optional; you can always hand-land a trout

unless you're fishing out of a float tube or boat. But a net makes the job easier, and also can make it less abusive to the fish. Quick insertion into a net, and a similar quick release, is better than the thrashing and flapping that some fish endure when they are hand-landed. The meshes of a net help you get a grip on a trout without squeezing it, so that you can unpin the hook and get the fish back in the water quickly, without harm.

The net should be large enough to hold the size of trout you expect to catch. Writers are often criticized for using tiny nets to make all their fish look big in pictures. My personal net is very small. Rick Hafele's is bigger, but sometimes not big enough. We were drifting the Deschutes the other day when a fellow hailed us from shore.

"You guys got a net?" he hollered. He turned out to be an old friend, Don Reardon, and he had a big fish on. Rick went ashore, stood next to Don's hooped rod, and got ready with his trout net. Don forced the fish to the surface.

Rick held the little net timidly, far away from the fish, and said, "Hey, that's a steelhead!"

"I know," Don said.

Rick finally got up the nerve to net the fish. He had to take it in several bites. When he got as much of it as he could in the net, its head was straight down and about a foot of tail still stuck out. The steelhead weighed six pounds.

You can clip your net to you if you like, but make sure you can release it quickly, with one hand. I prefer my net out of the way in the center of my back. A net retriever lets me reach a fish with it, and reels the net back into position as soon as I let it go. As always, things are most handy when they are least in the way.

The goal, when gearing up for fly fishing, is always to carry the least you can, while still possessing about your person everything that you know you'll need. Many of the peripheral items are nice to have when you want them. But the more experienced the angler, the more he seems to do without what he doesn't need, preferring instead to carry the necessities but leave home the luxuries.

Fishing light and unburdened is in itself a luxury.

Part II
Technique

1

The Basic Fly Cast

At one time, fly casting was said to be so difficult that only a few folks were qualified to master it. That's hardly true. More recently, fly casting is said to be so easy that anybody can master it in an hour. That's not true either. The truth lies in between; it doesn't take long to learn to cast well enough to take *some* trout. It takes longer than any of us have on earth to learn to cast well enough to take *every* trout. It's the journey in between, which truly has no end, that makes fly fishing for trout such an intriguing operation.

Casting a fly is neither physically nor mentally difficult. It's a pleasure when it's done right, a fearful tangle when it's done wrong. The cause for doing it wrong almost always lies in trying to cast farther than the caster's current abilities allow. The angler who has mastered the thirty-foot cast will get into trouble trying to extend it all at once to fifty feet; the person who can cast eighty feet without trouble might find himself in plenty of it if he suddenly decides to cast 100 feet.

Most trout are caught with twenty-five- to forty-foot casts, even by experienced fishermen who have no problems punching out sixty to seventy feet of line. The caster who learns to cast well *short,* and then learns the various techniques of presenting flies and manipulating their drift or float, will be a lot better fisherman than the person who learns to cast the whole line straight to the other side of a river, but hasn't learned what to do about it once it gets there.

Once you learn to cast short but right, it becomes easy to extend the cast in small increments until you can also cast long and right.

The movements that constitute a fly cast happen in a bit of a hurry; you can't loft your backcast, then spend a few minutes pondering your forecast before making it. There is an instant, which the rod and line and your hand tell you about, when it's the right time for the forecast, and that's when you must make it. The success of each movement in fly casting depends on the proper execution of the movement before it. You can't toss a wobbly backcast, then deliver a graceful and powerful forecast from it.

It is an interesting challenge to parse out the parts of a good cast and describe them, because of the speed of a cast and the way its parts unfold one upon the other. But isolating the separate movements is the best way to learn to cast right. It also makes learning seem less formidable, because when a cast is broken down there aren't very many movements in it. It's nice to see how easy it really is.

When you learn the separate parts of the basic casting stroke, you must put them together and execute them with vigor tempered by grace. Practice them on lawns and lakes and in fishing situations until you can cast without being conscious of it. It won't happen in an hour, or even in a few days, but there will come a time when your rod begins to report to you. It tells you when it is loaded, and the time is right to drive it into the backcast. It tells you when the line is straight in the air behind you, and it's time to start the forecast. When you reach this point your focus will shift to the trout, away from the rod, and you will be fly fishing, not just fly casting.

My friend Derek Sandoz took up fly fishing when he was thirteen. A summer later, when he was fourteen, I invited him to float and fish the Deschutes with me for three days. Rick Hafele, who fishes a nymph as well as anybody I know, was on the trip. So was Richard Bunse, who can coax dry flies into whispering seductive nothings into the ears of reluctant trout. I expected to have to take Derek under my wing, to teach him the rudiments of casting so that he might get a fly into a fish or two. The Deschutes is a river that held me off for a few seasons, and I suspected Derek was in for a frustrating few days.

I was wrong. Derek needed no instruction at all in casting. His outfit was a balanced beginner's combination from a manufacturer who has been around for a long time. He cast well with it, covering the water without trouble in that twenty-to-forty-foot range where we catch most of our trout on the Deschutes, even though it is a broad and sometimes brawling river.

Because Derek was able to cast without instruction, I was able to lean back against the boat and watch while Rick showed him some fine points of nymphing. He got into several fine rainbows in the first riffle we fished.

Later Richard put Derek over some selective noses that poked rhythmically through the surface, in a glass-surfaced run along the edge, under some alders. With minimal instruction Derek was at them, fishing dry flies. Nothing happened for a long time. Richard and I were far off in conversation when we heard a shout, looked up, and saw Derek playing a fish. He had to follow it seventy-five yards downstream through a difficult boulder garden. I followed Derek and hand-landed the trout in a back eddy; before I gave it up to him to hold and release, I stretched my hand along its side twice with enough left over to know the fish was just a bit shorter than eighteen inches.

Derek worked the fly out of the trout's jaw, and only then did I notice that it was a small nymph. "I thought you were fishing dry," I said.

"I was," he answered as he revived the fish. "But they wouldn't take a dry, so I changed to the nymph, and fished it just like a dry. The fish took it on the first good cast."

Because he had learned to cast well enough to cover fish, Derek was able to take advantage of instruction from the likes of Rick Hafele and Richard Bunse. I have a hunch it saved him several summers in his fly fishing journey. I asked him how he had picked casting up so well, in such a short time.

"By practicing in the back yard," he told me. That's my advice to you: practice in the back yard.

When you have reached the point of grace with a short cast, and discipline yourself to cast in control rather than ten feet beyond it, you will quickly master fly casting and make it fun. After you've mastered the basic stroke, then there are years to hone your skills and extend your casts. Be patient; fly fishing isn't going to go away tomorrow.

HAND POSITIONS

Whether you are right-handed or left-handed, your *rod hand* holds the rod and your *line hand* holds the line.

During the cast, the rod hand holds the cork rod grip with the fingers wrapped around it and the thumb lying along the back of it, opposite the reel. The thumb in this position helps you both aim the rod and power the cast. The rod tip goes where the thumb points; the line goes where the rod tip points. The grip should be firm, but not tense.

The proper rod hand grip has the thumb along the back of the cork, the fingers wrapped comfortably around it. J. L. Schollmeyer

After the cast, the thumb can drop down alongside the grip, or stay on top of the rod. When you hook a fish the thumb will wrap around the grip by itself, without your directions to do so.

As soon as a cast is dropped to the water, the line hand must deliver the line to the rod hand, draping it over the forefinger, on the underside of the grip, while keeping hold of the line below this point. This is a constant; the rod-hand forefinger picks up the line at all times with the exception of the cast itself, or when a fish is being played on the reel. It's a busy finger.

Pressure on the line between the fore- and middle fingers of the rod hand can be used to lock the line in place, or to let it slip in and out. Slack should never be allowed to form between the first guide, which is called the stripping guide, and the forefinger of the rod hand. Slack there causes problems when you have a hit: you raise the rod to set the hook, but all the rod movement can accomplish is the removal of the slack at its butt. The fish swims away while you fumble with the line, trying to get it tight. The same slack below the stripping guide causes problems in casting: you raise the rod to load it and make the cast, but nothing happens because the slack absorbs all the rod energy that should go against a tight, straight line.

During the cast, the line hand controls the line, holding it firmly while the rod is loaded and powered, letting line slip so it can shoot to extend the cast. The line hand does not relinquish its grip on the line after handing it over to the rod-hand forefinger, after the cast. The line hand loops the line over the busy forefinger of the rod hand, but does not let it go. The line hand draws line in, or lets it out over the forefinger of the rod hand, as the circumstances of casting and fishing the fly demand.

The line hand controls the retrieve, holding the line steady on a downstream fly swing, stripping line in for a fast retrieve, bringing it in with a hand-twist motion on a slow retrieve, or gulping it fast when an upstream cast onto a fast current brings the fly back toward the rod in a rush.

The line hand gathers line in loose loops during the retrieve, then feeds them one by one into the cast as line is extended, and frees them at the last instant to shoot out on the final delivery stroke. With short casts the loops are small and easy to control. With long casts they are larger, trail in the water if you are

After the cast is made, and the fly is fishing, the rod hand forefinger and the line hand combine to control the line throughout the drift or retrieve of the fly. J. L. Schollmeyer

wading, and often get unmanageable. These loops of line are one of the things you must learn to control with experience; never try to cast more line than you can control in your line hand.

When a fish hits the fly, the rod hand lifts the rod to set the hook. The rod-hand forefinger and the line hand clamp down to keep the line from slipping on the strike. If the fish is a big one and runs, the line hand instantly feeds line after the strike, letting it slip into the guides, with slight tension, until all the slack is out and the fish can be played from the reel. If the fish is a small one, it can be played by stripping in line with the line hand, locking it down with the rod-hand forefinger while the line hand gets a fresh grip near the rod hand to draw in more line. If the fish makes a run, line can be surrendered by the line hand. The rod-hand forefinger can be used to apply slight drag.

Whether the fish is big or small, the two hands should endeavor to control the line in such a way that slack is never allowed between the rod and the fish. A tight line keeps the hook drawn into the fish's jaw; slack allows it to work free.

The Basic Cast

The purpose of the basic fly cast is to get the fly out to the water in front of you, where a trout can get at it, in most fishing situations. The basic cast consists of the graceful weaving of fore- and backcasts. It is what we think about when we think about the poetic movements in fly fishing.

The basic cast begins with the rod pieced together, the line strung through the guides, a leader and fly tied on. When assembling the rod, align the guides and push the sections together firmly with your hands *close* to the ferrule. When separating it later, pull it apart with a firm grip and your hands at least a few inches *away from* the ferrule. When stringing the line, don't try to poke the leader tip through each guide. Instead, double the line and poke the loop through the guides. It's a lot easier to hold; if you let it slip, it won't slither back out in an instant, but instead will stop at the first guide and wait for you to get a new grip on it.

For practice sessions the leader should be short and stout, say, seven to eight feet, tapered to about .008, or 3X. The fly should be bright, so that you can see it in the air, and should have its

The proper stance in preparation for the basic casting stroke: elbow com- fortable, forearm straight, and feet positioned at a 45 degree angle across the cast. J. L. Schollmeyer

point cut off. An inch of fat fluorescent yarn makes an excellent fly, and won't hurt anybody if it is sent in a wrong direction.

The basic cast is best practiced on a lawn, though water is fine if you have some. Sorry, but it's wise to practice where you are not distracted by fish. You will want to start with the line extended twenty to twenty-five feet in front of you, and straight, by walking it out there, which is another advantage to starting on a lawn instead of a lake.

With your line out in front of you, assume the proper rod grip, thumb on top, and take hold of the line with the line hand a few inches from the rod hand. Point the rod at the line, and draw in any slack. Hold your elbow where it falls comfortably, down at your side and a few inches away from your body. Your forearm should be almost straight, and your wrist should be cocked downward to lower the rod point. Your feet should be positioned at about a 45-degree angle across the cast, so that you can turn your head and watch the mystery of your backcast unfold behind you.

The Backcast

To execute the backcast, lift the rod quickly until it is at an angle of about 45 degrees to the ground. Lift with your forearm; keep your wrist cocked. Now put on the brakes and think for a moment. You have done a couple of things. First, you have lifted the rod toward eye level and got it bent a bit. Second, you have taken every bit of slack out of the line and got it tugging straight against the rod tip and moving in your direction. It's the first part of every casting stroke, and it's called *loading the rod*. The rod is loaded when it is bent and the line is straight and pulling against the rod tip.

Now extend your line back out on the lawn.

Lift the rod quickly to 45 degrees again, to load the rod. Without a pause, and with a fast and strong movement of both your forearm and wrist, drive the rod back to a position slanted just a few degrees behind your rod-arm shoulder. Now put on the brakes again and watch your backcast unfurl. This is the *power stroke*, and it is brief but fast. It is the most important movement in fly casting.

Loading the rod is the first step in every fly cast. It serves to straighten the line, and to get it pulling tight against a rod that has the beginnings of a bend in it. J. L. Schollmeyer

The power stroke drives the rod through a short arc, but with much more speed and strength than the loading stroke requires. J. L. Schollmeyer

If the backcast goes straight over your shoulder and straightens into a line parallel to the ground, you did it right. If it goes high up into the air, you put on the power too soon. If it drives toward the ground, you put on the power too late. If you did it right the first time, it won't be long before you are giving me lessons.

The power stroke must be executed with strength. That is why it must use the arm *and* wrist, not just the wrist. There is simply not enough muscle in a wrist movement alone to cast a fly very far. For many years I was a wrist caster; until I freed up my elbow and put some arm muscle into my casts, I suffered a sore wrist every time I went fishing for more than an hour. Many tournament casters, and those who fish with the tournament casting stroke, keep the wrist locked, not using it at all. They will scold me for the way I describe the cast, but most of them are

If the power is put on too soon, the line shoots into a high backcast, which is perfect in many situations. If it is put on at the right time, the line straightens out behind you, almost level with the ground, or the water. If it is put on too late, the line is driven into the ground, or onto the water, behind you. J. L. Schollmeyer

experienced casters, and most of them started off casting the way I describe it because it is easier to learn, and also effective for all but tournament casting, which is not trout fishing.

The power stroke must be executed in the right sequence in the cast. It seems foolish to say that, since we've only talked about two movements so far. But it's common to get them backward, and it's good to think about getting them in the right order while only two movements are in the air. *Load the rod,* then *apply the power.* The loading movement is a long upsweeping lift of the rod, drawing slack out of the line and putting both rod and line in the right position for the power stroke. The power movement is brief but strong, almost a snap that drives the rod a short distance at a high speed.

Imagine the two movements in reverse order for a moment: first the power stroke, then the loading of the rod. If you apply the power while the rod is low and the line has slack in it, most power is wasted taking up slack; when the slack is taken up, the line is jerked awkwardly into the air; when the line is jerked into the air, the rod is still moving in its upward arc, so the line is flung towering above you instead of being extended straight behind you. Then the power stroke is followed by the loading movement, and all it serves to do is move the rod backward while the line is already traveling backward and upward. The rod undermines the line, and introduces slack into it that must be taken out on the forecast.

When the backcast is executed in proper order, with the rod loaded and then the power delivered, the momentum of the rod will carry it back behind the shoulder. But the power must stop with the rod tipped just a few degrees back, and if there is a third movement in the basic casting stroke, it is the *stop,* which is no movement at all. But it is very important. In fact, it is the most violated of the three movements in fly casting.

The idea is to throw the line straight back, parallel to the ground, in an unfurling loop. Any power put on the rod after it is past about 15 to 20 degrees behind your shoulder forces the tip into the downward part of an arc, and serves to drill your line into the ground behind you. If you are in a fishing position, that means you will either catch brush behind you, knock your hook point off on rocks, or slap the water and kill your cast.

The fly-casting movement is often described in terms of a clock face. The backcast should be loaded in the short arc from two back to one o'clock, powered from one up to twelve, and stopped there. Glance at your watch to imagine the proper stroke.

That three-part movement in the fly-casting stroke is central to a good cast: *load the rod, put on the power, stop the rod.* The stop is part of the snap of the power stroke, impossible to separate from it. But it is just as important as the start. It's true for both backcast and forecast. It would not hurt you now to practice the backcast for a while, watching the line straighten behind you and then drop to the ground several times before going on. If you work on it until the line drives back parallel to the ground, and then floats down toward the ground nearly level, you're going to remove a lot of potential problems from your future forecasts.

I mentioned that the stop is the most violated particle of the casting stroke. I have taught many casting classes over the years. After I give a thorough demonstration of the basic cast, it is the students' turn to cast. I warn them, just before they start, that my job for the rest of the class will be to walk up and down the line behind them and tell them not to drop their rods on the backcast.

The stop is just as important as the start in the basic casting stroke. It allows the line to begin unfurling in a tight loop, straight over your shoulder, rather than drilling into the ground, or drifting back in a lazy, open loop. J. L. Schollmeyer

There is far more to it than that, but that is still a lot of what I do. Ignoring the stop, and dropping the rod on the backcast, is the most common and most aggravating casting error.

Almost every student starts out with the rod pointed straight in front, powers it through a full arc overhead, and ends with it pointing straight behind. The line does its best to chase the rod tip all the way, but its energy is dissipated by its going wildly up, around overhead, and then down. No loop is ever formed. Just when the line thinks it is going to get a chance to rest on the ground behind the student, it is forced to whip through its wild arc toward the sky and then dash toward the ground in front of him, on an errant forecast.

The fly cast that does not stop when the rod is just past straight overhead will catch far more of whatever is behind you than it will of the trout that are out in front of you.

After the stop, the momentum of the rod will carry the tip back. The power stops when the rod is overhead; the rod then drifts back. That is the way it is supposed to happen. Let the tip drift back until the rod stands at approximately a 45-degree angle to the ground. Don't let it go beyond that line.

Let your arm drift back a few inches, following the rod, but without lowering the angle of the rod. This slight drift puts the rod into a position that allows you to load it on the forward cast. The *rod drift* is the fourth movement of the basic fly cast, and because of the laws of momentum it is one that more or less takes care of itself. You don't have to consciously drive your rod back; you just have to stop the power stroke when the rod is overhead, then let the rod follow the line into the right position for the forecast.

The Forecast

The first backcast started with the rod pointed almost straight out in front of you. Why shouldn't the forecast start with the rod at the same angle behind you? It's simple: your line was on the ground when you started the first backcast, and will be on the water when you are fishing. But the line should be straight and at rod-tip level, up in the air, when you start the forward cast.

The forward cast itself follows the exact sequence of the back-

In the last movement of the backcast, the rod is allowed to drift back slightly, into the 45 degree position that prepares it for the forecast, while the loop of line unfurls. J. L. Schollmeyer

cast. That is why I say that fly casting is actually very simple. There are only four movements within the cast: loading the rod, the power stroke, the stop, and the drift. But you only have to remember two of them: loading and powering the rod. The stop is part of the power stroke; the drift is a continuation of it caused by momentum.

Recall that a good forecast cannot be launched from the wobbly platform of a bad backcast. It is best to begin forecasting only after you have worked on backcasting until you can consistently cause the line to straighten behind you at approximately rod-tip level, and approximately parallel to the ground.

When the forecast begins, the line is straight, the rod is at a 45-degree angle, and your rod hand is about level with your shoulder. Your wrist, without any effort on your part, is already cocked slightly backward after it came out of its forward cock on the power movement of the backcast. You are now ready to make the two memorized movements of the forecast: loading the rod and punching in the power stroke.

To *load the rod* for the forecast, bring your forearm forward a foot or so without changing the angle of the rod. This forward movement takes up any slack that might be in the line, and it gets the rod started into its bend, exactly as it happened on the backcast.

The forward movement to load the rod must be made when the line is straight in the air behind you, or when the last of the loop is already turning over to straighten out. Start into the forward stroke too soon and it serves only to accelerate the speed with which the loop unfurls behind you. It will crack the whip. If you wait too long, the line will have collapsed toward the ground. This will cause few problems when you practice on a lawn, but it will cost you lots of flies if you carry the habit over onto the stream, where bushes lurk.

There is a correct moment for the forecast. If you watch the line unfurl when you practice, you will soon be able to correlate the correct feel—it's almost a tug—to the time when the line straightens out, and soon you will know when the moment is right without turning to watch.

The *power stroke* is the same almost abrupt snap of the forearm and wrist that powered the backcast. It starts with the rod at its 45-degree angle, and stops when the rod is a few degrees past straight up. Again, the power stroke is executed with strength and speed. It needs the muscles of the forearm. Imagine trying to

Load the rod for the forecast by driving it forward a foot or so. This movement removes any slack from the line behind you, and starts the rod into its bend. J. L. Schollmeyer

The power stroke for the forecast is executed with strength and speed. The rod is stopped when it is just past straight overhead, or the line will unfurl in an open, lazy loop. J. L. Schollmeyer

drive a nail while moving nothing but your wrist. You'd merely plink at it, which is fine if it's a tack. If it's a stout nail, you want some weight behind it.

A fly rod is a stout nail.

The timing of the *stop* is just as important as the proper start in the power stroke, and is actually an integral part of the power stroke. If the rod is driven much past the point where it is straight up, the tip goes into its downward arc and the line dives toward the ground in front of you. If you do this while you are fishing, the line piles into the water, and by the time the fly crashes to the water behind it all the trout are in Kansas. Stop the power while the rod is high so the forecast goes out straight and high.

For the first few forecasts, let the line straighten in front of you and then drop to the ground. You want to practice until you can achieve the same thing you achieved on the backcast: a loop that unrolls at rod-tip level. The line should come straight while parallel to the ground, then should float down toward the ground nearly level from the rod to the fly. If you get into the habit of

If the forecast is executed correctly, with the loading, power, and stop movements all made at the right moments, the line will unfurl before you in a tight loop, parallel to the water. J. L. Schollmeyer

letting the rod tip settle with the fly, then you will wind up in position to make the next practice backcast and forecast. You will also get a jump on preparing for the delivery stroke.

Weaving Fore- and Backcasts

It helps to practice with single back- and forecasts until you have them down almost perfectly, because mistakes in any part of the cast get multiplied in the next part. If you try to weave the line back and forth with continual casting before you can do it once well, each sequence will slightly magnify the mistakes made before it until your line gets out of control. Once a cast gets out of control, it is almost impossible to get it back into control. It's best to stop, then start all over.

But it won't be long before you are ready to carry your line in the air. Then each backcast must be a preparation for the next forecast, and each forecast must be a preparation for the next backcast.

To make a backcast from a forecast rather than from the ground, the forecast must end with the rod in a position from which it can be loaded for the backcast. To do this merely means adding the *drift* to the loading, powering, and stopping of the forward stroke. Let the rod follow the line forward after you have stopped the power. Do not let the rod tip drop below the 45-degree angle to the ground.

When the line is straight in front of you, then bring the rod back a foot or so to load it, without changing its angle. Again, this takes up the slack in the line, and begins to bend the rod.

Apply the power stroke to the rod, with the same quick and forceful movement you have used in all of the power strokes. Let the rod drift back while you watch the backcast unfurl. When the line is straight, load the rod and power it into the next forecast.

If you have practiced fore- and backcasts separately long enough to make them smoothly, you will have little trouble learning to carry several in the air in sequence. But you will run into problems if you try to hold too much line in the air at first. Each cast will collapse farther toward the ground before the line is straight. Again, it is hard to recover once a problem is installed in the cast. Stop the cast, reel some line in, and start over.

You're going to have kinks in your casting at first. It's best to get as many of them as you can worked out in situations where you won't be bothered by fish. The first problem you'll probably have

When weaving fore- and backcasts, each backcast becomes the preparation for the next forecast. . . . Dave Hughes

. . . and each forecast becomes the preparation for the next backcast. Dave Hughes

to deal with is that long and swooping arc of your rod overhead. I haven't met many casters who didn't start off driving the rod from straight in front to straight in back. The symptoms are a loop that isn't a loop, and the line falling far too low on the backcast. The solution is to stop the rod when it is 15 to 20 degrees past straight overhead, and let it drift through without power.

The second problem you will likely encounter is poor timing on the forward stroke. The symptoms are the snap of a cracked whip if you start forward too soon, a line that waffles toward the ground if you start too late. The solution is to watch your backcast unfurl a few times, until you've got the feel for the moment when the line is straight in the air behind you.

A third problem that haunts many, though not all, casters is timidity on the power stroke. My father, who has fly fished for fifty years, suffers this because he has always used a fragile bamboo rod, and thought that if he cast too hard with it, it would snap. When he switched to glass, and then graphite, for some of his fishing, he still held back, and the result was underpowered casts that were impossible to control. There is no way to break a rod by casting too hard with it unless it already has a flaw, or it is vastly overloaded by the line weight placed upon it.

A fourth problem is the one already mentioned: getting the

power stroke ahead of loading the rod. The symptoms are slack and lots of wobbly curves in the line. The solution is to get the parts of the cast in their proper order. One way to do that is to practice the movements without a rod in your hand. Forget the stop and drift; concentrate on a two-part movement of load and power back, then a two-part movement of load and power forward. By practicing without the rod, you will drill into your arm and wrist the idea that it is a two-part movement, even though there is no substantial pause between them.

GETTING LINE OUT

In most fishing situations, you lack a lawn on which you can walk to get the first twenty-five feet of line out. Instead, you accomplish it by shooting a little line on each forecast until you've got the amount out that will place your fly where you want it.

Start by stripping line from the reel and dropping it to the water at your feet. Remove the fly from its keeper, hold it by the bend so you don't get hooked, and pull as much of the line

To start a cast while fishing, begin with several feet of line stripped from the reel, enough out to get the leader knot beyond the rod tip, and the fly held by its bend in your line hand. Dave Hughes

through the guides as you can. If you can't pull far enough to get the leader knot and a couple of feet of line beyond the rod tip, reach up and get another grip without letting go of the fly, and pull more line out.

Now you are in position to do one of two things. First, you can flick your wrist to roll the line, leader, and fly into the air in a backcast, and then begin the basic cast with a forecast. Let a few feet of line slip through your line-hand fingers on each forecast, and soon you will have the right amount of line out to make your presentation.

Second, you can flick your rod-hand wrist forward to straighten the line, leader, and fly out on the water in front of you. Then make a backcast, follow with a forecast, and let some line shoot into the forecast before it falls onto the water. Pick it up again and shoot some more. In this manner you should be able to get enough line out to load the rod for a cast after two or three pickups.

The first method of getting line out, starting with a backcast, is more commonly used when fishing dry flies or unweighted nymphs and wets. The second method, starting with the line on the water in front of you, and using successive pickups to get some line out, works well when fishing heavy flies, or when fishing with very stiff rods. It requires more line beyond the rod tip before the rod is loaded enough to make much of a cast. The drag of the water on the line, as it is picked up, serves to load the rod until enough line to load it can be carried in the air.

When your line is out and you are fishing, you will need to lengthen it for each cast after the retrieve. The second method of picking it up is used. Water tension helps load the rod on the first pickup, after which enough line is almost always out to load the rod for backcasts and forecasts held in the air.

Shooting line is one of the hidden movements inside the fly cast that can cause some trouble at first. Like everything else, it requires precise timing; after the timing is learned, shooting line is easy. Line should be shot only after the power stroke has been stopped, normally on the forecast, though with lots of experience you will also be able to shoot line on the backcast. To this day, I rarely shoot line on a backcast.

Release for the line shoot should happen at the same time as the rod stop after the power stroke. The unfurling loop will draw

The easiest way to start a cast is to begin with a short backcast, then extend line on successive forecasts until you have enough out to make your presentation. Dave Hughes

line through your line-hand fingers. Let just enough line slip out to extend the cast a few feet. You will soon get the feel for how much you can shoot without overloading the next backcast. If your line-hand fingers release line while the power is still on the rod, the tension against the rod is suddenly lost. The rod springs out of its bend against slack line, and the cast collapses.

After the line is shot out, and the cast is delivered to the water, you will fish it out and then retrieve line for the next cast. When drawing line in during the retrieve, hold onto it every few feet so that it forms loops that dangle from your line hand toward the water. On long casts the loops will dangle in the water. Learn to gauge the size of the loops to the amount of line you can shoot back out on each forecast. When you have it down, you will typically gather two to three loops on your retrieve. The first is shot on the first forecast, the second on the next forecast, and the last, if there is one, on the delivery stroke.

For long casts, you might want to gather four or five loops, but they will sometimes swirl in the current and tangle, or tangle in your hand. If you gather lots of small loops, and try to shoot line with three or four of them still held in your line hand, they will often tangle on the way out. You should rarely make your final cast with more than a couple of loops dangling from your line hand.

One thing to work on, though not in any hurry, is keeping the number of backcasts to a minimum. At first you will be able to shoot only two to three feet of line on each forecast. But as you get your timing down better, you will be able to shoot more line. The more line you can shoot, the fewer backcasts you will need to make to extend your line back out to fishing distance. The fewer backcasts you make, the more time your fly spends on or in the water. Experienced fishermen, even steelheaders casting seventy feet over broad runs in big rivers, rarely use more than two or three backcasts to extend their line before the final shoot.

THE DELIVERY STROKE

Forecasting and backcasting is fine, but it doesn't get your fly onto the water where trout can appreciate it. When you've extended your line to the right distance, it is time to take aim and make the final delivery stroke.

Recall that the rod tip goes where the rod-hand thumb points, and the line goes where the rod tip directs it. You will greatly improve the accuracy of your casting if you subconsciously use your thumb as a sighting device. This is not unlike the way an archer sights when shooting arrows instinctively.

Accuracy also requests that the rod be held straight up and down. If the rod is canted, the unfurling loop will also be canted, and the fly will slice down at an angle to the water instead of drifting straight down toward it. In order to hit what you aim at, you will have to calculate that angle.

The delivery stroke is an extension of the last forecast. The loading, power, and stop movements do not change. But the rod tip is allowed to drift down as the line shoots out. Once the power stroke is complete, allowing the rod to drift will not affect the cast; the line is already under its own momentum. By the time the fly floats to the water, the rod should be pointed straight at it, level with the water. This puts you in a position to direct the drift of a nymph, follow the swing of a wet fly, or draw in line ahead of the float of a dry fly fished upstream.

Though there are specific times when a high rod is a help in guiding the drift of a fly, for example, when fishing a tumbling nymph right under the rod tip, most of the time a low rod will give you some leverage when it's time to pull the hook home into the jaw of a trout. If you try to set the hook with a high rod and slack in the line, you're far more likely to set yourself down behind you.

The delivery stroke leaves you in position to fish out the float or drift of the fly once it drops to the water. J. L. Schollmeyer

A final note on the delivery stroke: aim the fly about two to three feet above the water. If you aim it too high, at rod-tip level, it will be subject to wind drift, which will push it away from where you want it. It will also be more likely to float down on a pile of leader. If you aim too low, right at the water where you want the fly to land, it will either smack to the water, or drive across the top of it behind the disturbance of the unfolding line loop. You don't want your fly to surprise the fish like a motorboat arriving.

LOOP CONTROL

I mentioned in the chapter on rod selection that the primary goal of tackle selection is control. Control over the cast generally takes the form of control over the line when it is in the air.

The shape of the loop that you cast affects the distance of the cast and the delivery of the fly. A tight loop, a foot to three feet deep, cuts through the air like a knife. A tight loop is the goal of every distance caster because the narrow end of the loop is the only part of the line that must fight air resistance. The tighter the loop, the less the air resistance, and the longer the cast, given the same line speed.

An average loop, three to five feet deep, pushes against more air, and will not give quite the distance of a cast with a tight loop. But it is far easier to achieve and to manage in the air, and it will put out a fly to most reasonable fishing distances. It also makes it a little easier to control the delicate delivery of a fly, because things aren't happening quite so quickly out there at the end of the line.

An open loop, six or more feet deep, can be useful when you use two- and three-fly casts and don't want them arguing in the air. It also helps when you cast weighted flies and want the patient unfurling of an open loop.

The size of the casting loop is a function of rod action. The faster the rod, the tighter the loop. The slower the rod, the wider the loop. The size of the casting loop is also a function of the length of the power stroke. The shorter the stroke, the tighter the loop. The longer the stroke, the wider the loop. Loop control comes from learning to lengthen or shorten the power stroke.

A short power stroke results in a tight casting loop, good for casting control, ease, and when you need it, distance.

Tournament casters use rods that are very stiff, and casting strokes that are so short and quick they appear to be abrupt when you watch a cast. But tournament casters load the rod and execute the power stroke the same as the rest of us do; they just do it with lightninglike speed. Half of the secret is in how hard they stop the rod after turning the power off. Though it has its

A long power stroke results in a wide casting loop, all right in some situations, but usually at a cost in control, ease of casting, and in distance.

place in many kinds of fishing, I advise making the quest for a tight loop a lazy one. It seems to me that tight loops and distance casting have become obsessions among fly fishermen and some rod designers.

But loop control is a help in fishing, and learning to cast a tight loop is part of learning loop control, so don't back completely away from it. And distance casting has a place in trout fishing. It's just not the only place.

The way to learn loop control is to fiddle with your casting stroke when the fishing is slow, and watch how your fiddlings affect your loops. Before long you will be able to open and close them, to a certain degree, without being conscious of what you are doing to your casting stroke to make it happen. Again, you will be well along the road to good fishing when you begin to cast without concentrating on it.

Few fishermen learn to cast without dealing with lots of tailing, or closed, loops. This is a loop where the end of the upper portion of the line drops below the underportion of it. In other words, the fly and leader scoop under the line coming off the rod tip. When they cross they connect, and you must pull them in to get them apart.

Tailing loops arise from two primary causes. The first is getting the power stroke ahead of the loading movement. This is easy to

The tailing loop, in which the end of the line scoops under the middle of the line, and usually catches it on the way by, is a problem that nearly every caster has to solve. It is almost always the result of a problem in the casting stroke.

cure by taking the time to practice the casting movement for a few minutes without the rod in your hand, or with just the butt of the rod in your hand. Once you've got the sequence down again, your casting will iron itself out.

The second cause of tailing loops is trying to cast farther than your abilities allow. This is easy to cure: draw some line in, be patient, and extend your abilities before you extend your casts.

Extending your abilities in fly casting is basically a matter of improving the precision of your casting stroke. It takes practice. Past a minimal point, when you've learned to get twenty to thirty feet out on the water, you can get that practice while fishing.

CHANGING DIRECTION OF THE CAST

After the drift or swing of your fly is complete, it is rare that your line will lie in the same direction that you want it to be put out on the next cast. A wet fly or nymph fished on the swing is a perfect example: the drift ends far downstream from where it started, and you must make your next cast back upstream to the starting point. To do this, you've got to pick the line off the water and change its direction radically before the next delivery.

Changing direction is easy. Remember that the line follows the rod tip. You will be able to change the direction a bit on the pickup and first backcast by angling the rod toward the direction you want. But you won't get much change because the line won't come out of the water cleanly if you try to pull it out at a large angle. On the forecast, however, with the line in the air behind you, quite a change in the direction of the cast can be made. Merely point the rod where you want the cast to go, and the line will follow. If the needed change is too much for a single forecast, you can add more change on the next backcast, then deliver the fly where you want it on a final forecast.

If two backcasts are required to make the full change in direction, split the change and make half of it on each cast. If you try to make too much change on one cast, your line will tell you about your mistake by piling up all around you. It doesn't take long to get the feel for how much change in direction you can make on a single back- and forecast.

If you must change direction and reextend your line at the

same time, you might want to accomplish the change first. The shorter the line, the easier it is to change directions. Then you can extend your line with one or two extra backcasts. As you grow comfortable with both changing directions and shooting line, you will find it easy to do both on the same forecast. Many experienced wet-fly men, and most summer steelhead fishermen, can make one pickup of thirty to forty feet of line, change the direction of the forward cast back upstream, and shoot fifteen to twenty feet of line into the delivery without an extra backcast. This can result in casts to sixty feet with a single backcast.

Another use for the change-of-direction cast puts it at the delivery end of the cast instead of the pickup end. When you fish over trout holding in shallow water on flats, or cast over wary trout holding in the tiny pools of mountain creeks, the line passing overhead will spook every fish that sees it, and they will spook every fish that sees them. To prevent this, make your fore- and backcasts in a direction that keeps them out of sight of the fish. Then change the direction of the cast on the delivery stroke, so that only the leader covers the fish, and then only once.

2

The Roll Cast

I once thought sea-run cutthroats were unique among trout. They are in a way; they live in rivers that have access to the ocean. They drop downstream into estuaries, and feed boldly in rich pastures. They return to fresh water fat and strong, but used to using depth and darkness for cover. When they are in their native streams, sea-runs crouch along the shorelines, favoring deep, dark lies with little current and lots of sweeping branches to hide them from overhead.

Coastal sea-run streams are narrow, their banks backed close with alder trees and dense brush. Getting along them is difficult. Casting in the normal manner is almost impossible: there is rarely room to stretch out a backcast behind you.

For many years I had difficulty taking sea-runs. They were elusive then, and still are, but I spoiled most of my chances by sending out wading waves trying to get into a position from which I could use a basic cast to get a fly back under the brush. In my inexperienced youth I didn't know I was spooking the fish before I ever cast to them. I just assumed the fish weren't there.

In truth they had fled before me, or else they cowered where they were and refused to move when my casts pounced at them.

In the years when I first learned to roll-cast, I found that sea-run streams suddenly held much heavier populations of these stout trout. Strangely, they came from all the places I had always tried to fish before, which is to say the angriest places, the places most difficult to fish.

It did not take me long to discover that the same roll cast delivered flies to difficult lies on all trout streams. The populations of rainbows and resident cutthroats in the streams I had always fished suddenly nosed upward, also. So did their average size. When finally I got a chance to travel and to fish for them, I discovered that brown trout also loved to hover along undercut and brushy banks.

The roll cast is designed to put flies into the toughest places. Because of the nature of such lies, and the fact that other folks don't fish them much, the biggest trout are often found at the end of the shortest cast.

The roll cast is executed with the line on the water in front of the rod. Surface tension serves to load the rod, and this is a cast that can't be practiced on a lawn. If you do so, your best and most precise effort will accomplish no more than piling the line at your feet, and you will think you have failed.

The roll cast can be thought of as an extension of the basic cast. The power stroke is exactly the same. But the preparatory movements for the roll cast, in order to load the rod, are not at all like those made in the basic cast.

The roll cast is started with the line on the water in front of you, usually extended and at least reasonably straight. For purposes of practice you can get it out there using the basic cast as outlined in the last chapter. In later notes you will see how to get it out when brush behind prevents the basic cast, which is when you will want to resort to the roll cast in fishing conditions.

The roll cast should be short, not more than twenty to thirty feet at first. The same principle that you practiced with the basic cast is very important: learn to do it short and right before you try to do it long. The roll cast is a useful tool for most trout fishermen in the range from fifteen to forty feet. I do know steelhead fishermen who use it consistently out to forty-five and fifty feet.

Roll-casting is easiest with long rods because they lift the line higher off the water. The stiffer the rod, within reason, the better it will deliver the punch of a brisk power stroke down the line. Slow rods work, but not quite as well. That is why graphite rods, with their light inherent weight, roll-cast better than heavier fiberglass and bamboo rods.

Weight-forward lines are fine for roll casts out to about forty feet, the length of the heavy taper plus the leader. Since this is as far as you will want to roll-cast anyway, in most situations, the weight-forward taper is just as effective as the double-taper. Those who want to make longer roll casts choose double-taper lines because the light running line behind a weight-forward taper will not lift the heavier line off the water and drive it into a hoop. Lee Wulff's long belly lines, with their forty-foot front tapers, roll-cast very well, and far enough for anybody. His Triangle Tapers, with heavier line constantly bossing the lighter line in front of it, are premier roll-casting lines.

The roll cast is limited to the floating line, though it is possible to force ten feet of a wet-tip line to the surface, then put out a quick, short roll cast with it. Full-sinking lines, wet heads, and wet bellies are almost impossible to roll-cast. The floating line executes a roll cast far better if it is kept clean, so that it rides on the surface its entire length.

It is easiest to roll-cast small flies, and unweighted flies. Weighted nymphs and large streamers are sometimes too deep in the water to be drawn to the surface by the time the roll-cast hoop has reached the end of the leader, which is also at the trailing end of its power. The line usually rolls out past the leader, but leaves the leader stuck back behind with the fly.

If you must roll-cast a weighted fly, it sometimes takes two casts, the first extending the line and bringing the fly to the surface, the second following quickly behind the first to roll out another hoop before the fly has a chance to sink more than inches. The second hoop plucks the fly out of the water and loops it over to the extent of the leader. If the leader is eight feet long, that means a difference in the cast of about fifteen feet, which in roll-casting is the difference between a killing cast and no cast at all.

The hand grip on the rod, for a roll cast, is exactly the same as the grip for the basic cast: the thumb should be aligned down the back spine of the cork grip, the fingers wrapped around the underside. The line hand holds the line tightly. If it slips, the cast collapses.

To load the rod, start with the line on the water in front of you and the rod level, pointed down the line. It is the exact position taken before the pickup for the first backcast in the basic cast.

Lift the rod tip upward in a smooth sweep, just fast enough to pull the line toward you without lifting it off the water. Bring the rod all the way back to the 45-degree position behind you, as if you were preparing for a forward power stroke, which is exactly what you are doing. Cant the rod slightly outward, just enough so the line passes to the outside of the rod as it comes past it. If you let the line come to the inside of the rod, the power stroke rolls it out and the hoop gets hung up in your armpit. There's no fish there.

The line is now sliding over the surface toward you. Pause for a moment, holding the rod poised in position for the power stroke. Just as with the basic cast, there is a precise moment when it is time to make the forward stroke. In the basic cast, the time was right when the line was straight in the air behind you. In the roll cast, the time is perfect when the line has followed the rod tip and formed a curve that hangs *behind* the rod, sweeping evenly down to meet the point where the line enters the water.

If the forward stroke is pushed before the line has fallen behind the rod, it does not accept more than a part of the power. The result doesn't form a hoop, or get the fly very far. If you wait too long, the line draws all the way in under the rod and hangs straight. It doesn't accept the power of the forward stroke well. Even worse, the line loses the tautness that surface tension has given it as it is drawn in. This surface tension is what loads the rod. Cast after the line has lost its momentum toward you across the surface, and you are casting with slack in the line. The result is the same as making the basic casting stroke with slack in the line: the movement of the rod serves to take up the slack instead of accelerating the line through the air. The cast is killed.

The proper timing for the forecast is the moment when the line has dropped behind the rod tip and formed a curve down to where it enters the water. At this moment, your rod is cocked at 45 degrees, and the line is curved behind the rod but still sliding toward you across the surface.

The rod is "loaded" for the roll cast power stroke when the rod tip is at a 45 degree angle behind your shoulder, and the line has formed an even curve down to the water. Dave Hughes

The power stroke is driven forward with the same movement used in the basic casting stroke. The wrist and forearm put on the power with a movement that is almost a snap. *The power is stopped at the same point it is stopped in the basic cast,* when the rod is just a few degrees past straight overhead. If the power is driven very far past the point when the rod is straight up, it causes the same problem it caused in the basic cast: it drives the line down toward the water. In the case of the roll cast this downward force drags the hoop down with it. The long power movement also opens up the size of the hoop, just as a long power stroke in the basic cast opens up the casting loop, making it less efficient because it is forced to cleave more air.

The goal of the roll cast is a small hoop of line running out, pulling the line off the water as it goes. It should not be a ball of line running across the surface; instead it should be in the air, lifting the line ahead of it up to it. The way to achieve this hoop of line traveling through the air is to send it off with a quick, sharp power stroke. Again, the *stop* is just about the most important part of the cast.

As with the basic casting stroke, the power must be stopped when the rod is still almost straight overhead, in order to form

The power stroke in the roll cast is the same short stroke used in the basic cast. The most common error is making a long and forceful stroke that drives the line in an open arc down into the water instead of in a tight hoop through the air.

the proper hoop. But as soon as the hoop is formed you can let the rod tip drop down into the position you want it for the delivery of the fly, and in order to have your rod in the correct position to fish the fly once it is on the water. Again, a high rod during the drift of the fly, or during the retrieve, is usually a disadvantage, especially if a fish takes the fly.

Each roll cast is normally delivered to the water and fished out. There is no fore- and backcasting in roll-casting. So each roll cast becomes a delivery stroke. The rod is dropped parallel to the water, usually while the hoop is still unfurling above the water. This is the way it should be done, but it leads to a tendency to drive the rod all the way into the delivery position. This is the key cause for weak roll casts.

The short power stroke, with an abrupt stop, forms the best hoop, and results in the longest cast, with the most precise presentation of the fly at the end of it. The rod follows the line, drifting down into the delivery position, while the hoop rolls out.

The roll cast should end with the rod dropping into position for the presentation, and the hoop of line rolling out to turn the leader over. Dave Hughes

GETTING LINE OUT

The roll cast requires surface tension to load the rod. It requires some line on the water in front of the rod. But if you were in a position to use the basic cast to get that first few feet of line out there, it's unlikely you would choose to use the roll cast to complete the cast.

There are two ways to get enough line out to get up some surface tension for a roll cast. The first is almost the same way it's done in the basic cast: take hold of the fly by the bend, then pull the leader and four to five feet of line beyond the tip guide. Now you can make a simple flip forward that is a truncated roll cast. Let go of the fly at the same time, and the line will straighten in front of you. Now strip a few more feet of line, make another roll cast, and let the stripped line shoot into the cast. Two or three such strips might be needed to get enough line out to make the delivery cast.

The second, and sometimes easier, way to get line out for the roll cast is to start with four to five feet of line beyond the rod tip, with the fly held by the hook bend in your line hand. Strip several feet of line off the reel. Now lower the rod tip, dropping the line that is beyond it to the water, and wiggle the rod tip

The easiest way to get the first few feet of line out for a roll cast is to wobble your rod tip back and forth, shaking line onto the water beneath the rod tip. Then roll it out. Dave Hughes

briskly back and forth. The tension of the fly in your hand and the line on the water serves to draw the stripped line through the guides. It lands in a zigzag pile under the rod tip, but a roll-cast movement will loft it and straighten it in front of you.

The amount of line out will still be short of what you need for your delivery. Strip more line off the reel, wiggle the rod back and forth again to get the line through the guides, then roll it straight out in front of you.

For the delivery stroke, draw the last line you need off the reel, wiggle it onto the water, and roll it into the final cast. You can also shoot a few feet of line into a roll cast. Shooting line into a roll cast requires the same timing used in the basic cast: you must release the line at the instant the hoop draws it out. If you release it too soon, you dampen the formation of the hoop, and kill the cast. If you let go too late, the hoop rolls out without drawing any line behind it.

If you are using the roll cast with an upstream dry, or with the kind of presentation that requires a retrieve, then you will have to reextend the line for each subsequent cast. You can choose between the two methods: wiggling the line beyond the rod tip, and rolling it out, or rolling the line that is already out, and shooting line behind it. A combination of the two might work best: wiggle out a few feet of line, roll it out, and shoot a few more feet behind it.

CHANGING THE DIRECTION OF THE CAST

As in fishing with the basic cast, your fly at the end of a drift or swing made by a roll cast is seldom where it was when you started. You must then combine extending the line for the next cast with changing direction back to where you want to deliver the fly.

If you fish from a position that takes the fly downstream on your rod-hand side, changing direction is easy. You merely make your first roll so that it roughly splits the angle that you must cover to get your fly back to where you want it. The second roll completes the change in direction and also becomes the delivery stroke that puts the fly where you want it for the next drift or swing.

If it is necessary to extend line at the same time you change direction, then you can either wiggle or shoot a few feet into each roll cast. It will not have much effect on your ability to change direction unless the cast is a long one: forty feet or more. If that is the case, it might take three or even four rolls to get the line back out and change its direction. But that should be a rare case.

Most of the time, the roll cast made off the weak shoulder should be used to put the line into a position where it can be lifted into a roll cast off the strong shoulder. Dave Hughes

When casting from the side of the stream that causes your rod arm to cross your body while following the swing of the fly, it's a little harder to change direction for the next presentation. But the principle is the same: Make rolls that split the angle and extend the line until the delivery stroke puts the fly where you want it.

The first roll must be a backhand cast that is executed with the rod above your off shoulder. Loading the rod requires the same lifting movement that draws the line toward you and cocks the rod at the right 45-degree angle, but this time over the line-hand shoulder. The roll is uncorked at the same correct moment, when the line has drawn a curve behind the rod. The power stroke must be the same quick and strong movement. Because of the position of your arm, this will be a wristy stroke, and won't have the power behind it that a normal roll cast owns.

The goal of the first roll should be to get the line upstream and into a position on the water from which you can make a normal roll cast. In other words the first roll, off the line-hand shoulder, will be weak but should bring the line above the rod hand. It might then be necessary to use an extra roll to extend the line and finish changing direction. A cast that requires two rolls off the rod-hand shoulder will usually require three when starting off the weaker shoulder, the first serving to get the line over to the stronger side.

Roll-casting with the wind on your rod-hand side is damned difficult. The wind pushes the loop into your body. The backhand roll, off the weak shoulder, then becomes the best way to deliver the fly. Some of your power will be lost because of the awkward position of the casting arm, but still you should be able to roll out twenty to thirty feet of line with quite a bit of practice. If you can position yourself so the wind aids your cast, you might be able to get off a better cast backhanded than you could forehanded.

ROLL-CASTING IN TIGHT SITUATIONS

Much of fly-fishing literature is devoted to the old bow-and-arrow cast. It can be useful where you are surrounded to an extreme. Grip the fly by its bend, draw it back until you have put a bit of arc into the rod, then aim and flick it out.

The bow-and-arrow cast is only useful for a cast about the

length of your leader. It can pop a fly into a pocket that is right in front of you, but it must be the kind of pocket that you can stalk to within eight to ten feet. There are, in truth, few such situations. It is much more common to want to cast twelve to twenty feet with a wall of brush behind you. In this kind of position the *half-roll cast* is far more useful.

I fish a lot of tiny streams. I often creep to the edge of a plunge pool, then want to place the fly on the surface of the water as if it just appeared there. Even if the pool happens to have room for a backcast, which is seldom, I don't want to loft my line because the fish are so close they will see it in the air. Instead of the bow-and-arrow cast, which would not get the fly the required distance, I grip the fly by its bend, wiggle a few feet of line onto the water, or even onto the ground, under the rod tip, then make a single roll that does not carry the line behind me. The surface tension of the line on the water is sufficient to load the rod. If the line lies on the ground, its weight will still load the rod for a cast of fifteen to twenty feet.

Because this cast is made so quickly, and the line does not go above the fish, the fly seems to appear on the pool as if by magic. Often trout respond at the instant the fly lands, almost as if they were waiting for it. Of course they were; that's their job, lying in wait for things that fall to the surface. The quickest trout get the most, and are apt to be the fattest. You will often take the largest fish from a pool with this first short cast.

ROLL-CAST PICKUP

When talking about the basic cast, I mentioned that one of the movements that must be executed with it is the pickup and extension of the line after an upstream dry-fly cast, when the fly has drifted down toward you, and the line hand has drawn in lots of line. Though this pickup can be done by drawing the line back over your shoulder for a normal backcast, this pulls the line in the same direction it is already traveling – toward you – and can be awkward to accomplish, especially in a fast current. An alternate method, one that most experienced fishermen use without even thinking about it, is the roll-cast pickup.

The roll-cast pickup is a simple motion that puts the line

straight into the air in front of you, in position for the backcast and then delivery stroke. It has the advantage of rolling the line off the water quietly, rather than ripping it off as a backcast often does. It also plucks the fly off the water straight up, again instead of ripping it off the water and frightening all the fish.

To execute the roll-cast pickup, stop drawing in line with your line hand when the fly has reached what you feel is the end of its effective float. Instead of drawing in more line, begin lifting the rod tip, paralleling the pace of the drifting line. When the rod has reached the 45-degree position over your shoulder, hold it a moment while the line drifts far enough to form the curve beneath the rod. Then execute the roll-cast power stroke. Most of the time the amount of line out is short, and the power stroke is little more than a quick forward flick that tosses out a hoop, lifts the line, the leader, and then the fly.

When the fly leaves the water, make a backcast, then execute the basic cast as if it had started normally.

3

Slack-line Casts

When fishing dry flies to a rising trout, especially on smooth currents, you should always strive to show the fly to the fish first, ahead of the line and leader. If you wade into a casting position that forces you to false-cast over the fish, or to drop the line over it in order to deliver the fly upstream from its lie, the trout will most likely wag its tail in disapproval and dart away.

Casting downstream to a rising trout always lets you show the fly first. But the downstream dry-fly cast presents a problem that is almost as large as lining the trout. The problem is *drag*. If the delivery is made with a straight line and leader, the fly is instantly at the end of its tether. It hangs there and leaves a wake, which is something the trout has never seen an ordinary insect accomplish. The result is the wagged tail of a departing trout.

The solution to the downstream cast is simple: install some slack in the line and leader, and the fly will float freely downstream ahead of them. If the fly is right, the leader is fine enough to give it freedom, and the presentation is made when the fish is ready to make its next take, the result will usually be a confident rise to the fly.

There are three ways to execute the slack line cast. With some casting and fishing experience, there is an infinite number of ways to combine them to fit the fishing situation.

THE PARACHUTE CAST

The *parachute cast* is an extension of the basic cast. Line is worked out with normal fore- and backcasts. A few extra feet of line are extended, more than are needed to reach the fish. Because extra line is carried in the air, the cast will be slightly overpowered compared to the power that would normally be necessary to make the cast to the distance required.

The variation from the basic cast takes place in the delivery stroke. The rod is driven forward on the last forecast with a strong power stroke. Then the rod is stopped abruptly, and not allowed to drift through behind the line, as it would be in a normal forecast. The tip is not allowed to drop, as it would on a normal delivery stroke. Instead, the rod is held almost straight up, but the rod hand drops from shoulder height to belt height.

As a result of the overpowered foreward cast, and the abruptly stopped rod, the line recoils softly toward the rod tip. The energy of the recoil forms a series of narrow S-turns down the length of the line and into the leader. Because the delivery stroke is finished with the rod held straight up, the line forms its curves at rod-tip height and floats to the water gently.

Dropping your rod hand vertically, with the rod held straight up, gives you several feet of extra drag-free float. As the S-turns work their way out, and the line starts to follow the fly downstream, you can drop the rod tip in an arc to follow the line downstream. When all of the rod length has been used up, you can extend your arm and get even more float. If you are casting with an 8-foot rod, and own a two-foot arm, you get ten extra feet of drag-free float in addition to that given as the S-turns straighten out.

It would be possible to perform the parachute cast without holding your rod vertically and dropping your rod hand. If you made an abrupt rod stop, then lowered the rod tip in the fashion of a normal delivery stroke, the S-turns of the line would still form and float to the water. But you would have nothing to do with the rod then, except to hold it still. Drag would immediately

The parachute cast drops a series of "S" turns to the water. With the rod held back you can lower it and follow the drift of the fly, extending its free drift. J. L. Schollmeyer

set in at the back end of the line, under the rod top, and the fly would get only a few feet of free float before the drag was transferred to the end of the leader.

The float will not always be as drag-free as it appears from your distant view, back at the rod butt. Out where the fly is about to arrive in front of the fish, there are lots of tiny conflicting threads of current that you can't see. They affect the drift of the fly just the same, and the trout can see the tiny tuggings they create. The drift of the fly will be free only so long as there is still slack in the leader itself. When the leader comes straight between the fly and the end of the line, drag will set in. It is important to practice this cast, and all of the slack-line casts, until the S-turns are reasonably even in both the line and the leader.

It is also important, when using the parachute cast and fishing over selectively rising trout, that the tippet be long and limp and the right diameter for the fly. Two feet is about the minimum-length tippet; five feet is not too long if the surface is glassy. If the tippet is too stiff for the fly, it will boss it around on the current no matter how much slack you contrive in the cast.

On smooth currents, try to place the fly as close as you can above the position of the rising fish. This keeps the float of the fly short, and takes advantage of the early portion of the drift that you know will be drag-free.

The place to take advantage of the full extension of a long downstream drift is on riffled water. The downstream cast often offers a better dry-fly drift in fast water than the upstream cast. Trout are sometimes shy of the line, even in fast water, but tendrils of current and unseen drag are not such great problems in that kind of water. The slack-line parachute cast, followed by lowering your rod tip and extending your arm, can give you fifteen to twenty feet of effective float in a riffle.

The parachute cast is effective over most of the range of dry-fly fishing, from fifteen out to about fifty feet. Beyond that, it is harder to use because the cast that would lay sixty feet of line on the water in curves would be an eighty-foot cast if the line were straight. I don't know about you, but I have sufficient troubles delivering sixty-foot casts with all of their tricks removed.

An effective variation of the parachute cast is what I will call the *towering cast*; I haven't seen it described or named. It is simple to execute. Begin with normal fore- and backcasts, but extend some extra line into the cast. On the delivery stroke, tilt the plane of the cast upward so that it ends high above the water: higher than the rod tip. Stop the rod as usual after the power stroke, but not abruptly as in the parachute cast. Now drop the rod tip slightly, and follow the descending line with the rod by lowering your rod hand from your shoulder to your belt or even lower. The rod should descend with its tip pointed up at an angle toward the falling line, as if you were lowering a rifle from your shoulder to your side while keeping it pointed at whatever it was you still might want to shoot.

The result of the towering cast is almost the same as the parachute cast: the line descends, almost sliding backward toward you, and forms S-turns as it drifts to the water. At the end of the cast the line lies on the water in curves, and the rod is held at your hip, still aimed down the line.

The drag-free drift of the fly, using the towering cast, will be short, just three to about five feet. The cast is best used when you want a series of short floats, and want to lift the fly immediately for the next cast. It works best on casts of thirty feet or less, followed by a quick roll-cast pickup and a single backcast before the next towering delivery.

The towering cast is an excellent method for working your way down a slightly rumpled run or a riffle, covering all the water with adjacent floats. The method and its pickup are a bit too brusque for use on glassy currents, over finicky fish.

THE WIGGLE CAST

The second method of delivering a fly to the water ahead of a slack line calls for wobbling the rod on the delivery stroke. It is the cast most commonly used to achieve a drag-free downstream drift. Mel Krieger called this the *wiggle cast* in his beautiful book *The Essence of Flycasting* (Club Pacific, 1987).

The line is extended for the wiggle cast in the normal manner, with basic fore- and backcasts. A little extra line is fed into the last forecast, enough to make up for the slack you will throw into the cast. The delivery stroke is made as usual, but aimed a little higher than the two to three feet above the water called for on a normal delivery. About halfway between the water and rod-tip height is about right.

As the line extends in the air, on the final cast, lower the rod tip behind it as usual on the delivery stroke. While the line is still straightening out, wobble the rod vigorously back and forth. This method installs a series of S-turns into the line, just as the parachute cast does. It is much easier to gauge the distance of the wiggle cast, and place the fly precisely where you want it. That and the ease of learning it are its main advantages.

The wiggle cast has a couple of disadvantages. First, the S-turns in the line start at the rod tip, and work their way out toward the fly, being wider in the back than they are at the front. Second, the wiggles in the line often poop out and fail to reach into the leader. The wiggle cast is more accurate than the parachute cast, and easier to execute, but it does not distribute the slack as evenly down the line and leader on a medium or long cast.

The wiggle cast is most useful for fishing close, thirty feet and under, where you can coax the S-turns all the way down to the leader. It works best when you are stalking fussy trout, where accurate placement of the fly is demanded. It works especially well over clear and smooth currents; the lower rod angle of the

The wiggle cast is the easiest of the slack line casts, and in many situations the most effective. J. L. Schollmeyer

delivery stroke is less likely to disturb fish than a line cast at rod-tip height, or towering far overhead before drifting to the water. Remember, when you cast downstream, the trout face upstream, into the current, and will see the line if it comes into their cone of vision above the water.

THE BOUNCE CAST

The final form of the slack-line cast, the *bounce cast*, is a variation of the parachute cast that is easier to execute. It is a workable cast in most fishing situations. With practice it works well in all directions: downstream, across-stream, and even when you want to be sure you have slack in your leader on an upstream cast.

The bounce cast begins with normal fore- and backcasting. A little extra line should be extended and carried in the air to compensate for the curves that are about to result. When the line is measured and aim taken, you are ready for the delivery stroke.

The delivery should be made high, at least halfway between the water and rod-tip height, higher than that on any cast forty feet or over. The final power stroke should be stronger than usual, so the line straightens in the air with plenty of momentum propelling it.

When the line is straight in the air, or almost so, draw back sharply on the rod, putting the *bounce* into the bounce cast. This should be a short, sharp movement. You don't want to draw the line into the beginnings of a backcast; you just want to stun it a bit, so it recoils into a series of small curves from fly to rod tip, just before dropping to the water.

The advantages of the bounce cast over the parachute cast and wiggle cast are several. It is easy to do, once you've practiced enough to get the feel for the right amount of bounce at various line lengths. It is a single movement at the end of the cast, so the rest of the cast is simply the basic fly cast. It puts the S-turns all the way down the line and leader, rather than just at the back of them. It can be done on a long cast or a short one, as long as you stay within the limits of your casting ability.

The one disadvantage of the bounce cast is inaccuracy. Because it is often used when casting across stream, to rising trout, it is a bit hard to calculate the extension of line, and degree of bounce, so that the fly lands and floats exactly down a narrow line of drift. This is not a problem if you are casting to a pod of trout rising in an area of water. It is a problem if you are trying to cover a specific fish that refuses to move from its feeding lane.

Three things will help you solve this problem of calculating windage. The first is practice, for which there are no substitutes in learning to fly-fish. The second is wading into a position that allows the shortest cast possible. The shorter any cast, the easier it is to calculate all of its factors. The third is to work your early casts to the near side of the fish. If you make your mistakes short of the fish, you won't put the fish down while getting its range.

The ease of the bounce cast, and the fine way it puts curves into the line, sometimes compensates for its inaccuracy. The low delivery angle of the wiggle cast sometimes offsets the disadvantage of the shorter drag-free float. The accuracy of the parachute cast can cancel the disadvantage of its difficulty and its limitations to the downstream direction.

You will be a better fisherman if you can make all of the slack-line casts, and choose among them, or even combine them, depending on what the water and the trout require.

4

The Reach Cast

The reach cast was first outlined in Doug Swisher's and Carl Richard's book *Fly Fishing Strategy* (Crown, 1975). The cast is most useful for extending the drag-free drift of a dry fly when fishing straight across the current, or across- and downstream. It is not a difficult cast. Once it is in your mix of casting tricks, you will find yourself using it often, and applying it to other casts as well.

The reach cast has its roots in fishing situations that had to be solved with innovative line control techniques. The problem to solve: trout rising across several feet of current from the caster. The currents in such a situation often conflict. If the cast is made with a straight line and leader, drag sets in at once. If the cast is made with S-turns of slack, the fly gets a short free float, but the line soon bellies downstream, tugging the fly after it.

The solution to extending the effective drift of the fly on a cross-stream cast lies in rod and rod-hand movements similar to those employed to solve the same problem in the parachute cast. In the parachute cast, the rod ends in the vertical position, with the line and fly downstream; dropping the tip and then extending the arm to follow the drifting line lengthens the drift by several feet. The reach cast uses similar maneuvers to extend the drift on a cross-stream cast.

The reach cast begins with normal fore- and backcasts that measure, and carry in the air, the amount of fly line needed to cover the line of drift upon which you want to place the fly. Aim is taken for the delivery stroke, and the cast is made so that the line straightens toward its target. The departure from the basic cast begins there.

The movement that makes a reach cast begins as the loop of the forecast unfurls, while the line is still in the air. Before the line begins to settle toward the water, simply lay the rod over in the upstream direction. It should end up parallel, or nearly so, with the surface. At the same time you lay the rod over, reach as far in the upstream direction as you can, extending the arm to its fullest length. If upstream is on your rod-hand side, you will get slightly more stretch than you will if upstream is on your line-hand side. In the latter cast, tip the rod over and reach across the front of your body with the rod hand. Lean into the cast and you'll get an extra couple of feet of free drift.

As I mentioned in the first chapter on casting, the line goes where the rod tip directs it. In the reach cast, the line and fly go where the power stroke aims them, which is right to the point where you want them to land on the water. But the back of the line follows the rod tip when you lay the rod over. By the time the fly and then the leader and line behind it all settle to the water, the line extends in a straight line from the rod tip, off to the side, instead of extending in a straight line from you, the caster.

As the fly begins its drift, you can now follow it with the rod, and the result is the same as feeding slack line into the drift. Continue to follow the drift by reaching the rod across your body, and end by extending the rod and rod arm as far downstream as you can. The reach cast can extend the float of a dry fly fifteen feet.

When executing the movement of the reach cast, timing is crucial but also easy. If the rod is tilted over while the power stroke is still directing the line, the line will follow the new

In the reach cast, you lay the rod over in the upstream direction, and extend your arm with it. As the fly begins its drift, you follow it with the rod, extending the free drift by several feet. If you combine the reach with a bit of a wiggle cast, it will enhance the drift even more.

direction of the rod. The cast will end up somewhere downstream of where you want it, probably bonk on the head of the fish, or even behind it. If the rod is laid over just as the fly settles to the water, the reach will redirect only a few feet of the back of the line, rather than all or most of it. The result will be an instant downstream belly in the line, and immediate drag on the fly.

The rod must be laid over after the forecast has delivered its power, but before the line has gotten to where it is going. On paper it sounds like you've got to time it to the split second, and make the move in a hurry. On the water it's a patient movement, delivering the power stroke, then letting the rod tilt slowly over while it follows its normal momentum forward. The rod reaches and the arm extends at a smooth and gentle pace. If it is done abruptly, the quick movement of the rod tip will crank a dogleg into the line. The result, again, will be a downstream belly and drag. Execute the reach cast, as you do most of the casts in fly fishing, with rhythm and grace.

The reach cast extends the drift of the fly from the back end of the cast, where the angler stands. The line is still placed on the water straight, and the problem of conflicting currents out where the leader lies is not solved at all. If there are no conflicting currents, then there are no problems. The straight-reach cast will do what wonders must be done. But the cast is designed to cross currents, and it is fairly rare that the currents don't travel at different speeds. To be truly effective, the cast is better if you can insert some slack into the end of the line and the leader. The best way to get some slack out there where you need it is to combine the reach cast with a form of the slack-line cast. You could do it by wiggling the rod as you lay it over, but this has the same inherent problem it has when the wiggle cast is used as a slack-line cast: it puts more S-turns back toward the rod than it does out toward the fly. The parachute cast won't work because your rod can't be held vertically and laid over at the same time.

The solution is employment of a slight bounce as the rod is laid over. If the rod is stopped at the end of the power stroke and drawn sharply back a bit before the rod is tipped over, the following movement of the rod tip will serve merely to take the slack back out of the rear end of the line. It will land on the water with a belly already in it. If the rod is laid over in the same patient arc that puts the reach into the cast, then drawn back sharply just before it settles to the water, the result will be a series of equal S-turns down the line and into the leader.

In order to add the bounce to your cast, you've got to add enough line in the air to compensate for the curves in the line. This is the same principle applied to any of the slack-line casts, and it becomes easy to calculate with practice.

The bounce requires an extra movement, and complicates the casting stroke. But it is not difficult to learn after you have both the reach cast and the bounce cast practiced enough that you can perform them without thinking about it. Combining them becomes automatic, and the combination of the reach and bounce casts is one you will use constantly when fishing over selectively rising trout.

5

Positive- and
Negative-curve Casts

There are many times in fly fishing when a direct presentation will frighten the trout you hope to take. You won't take many frightened trout. A lot of what you learn in the study of trout techniques is devised to get a fly in front of a fish without the fish discovering that the fly is attached to a leader and a line and you.

Positive- and negative-curve casts were first designed only to place dry flies upstream around obstacles, to lies that the angler couldn't get into position to reach any other way. Why is that true? Because most other ways are better. Curve casts at their best are slightly unpredictable. Their successful execution depends on a coming together of factors that are difficult to control.

Curve casts are a last resort for getting around obstacles, but they are still marvelous casts if there is no other way to get a good drift above a rock in the current. You might achieve that good drift on every other cast, or every third or fourth cast, but you're still going to increase your take of trout considerably. Trout love to hang out above obstacles in the current. The angler who can present an occasional fly to where they can get it will do better than the angler who must look at the place, then shrug his shoulders and trudge on to the next good lie.

In modern trout fishing there are other excuses to use curve casts. More people fish over insect hatches now, on smooth currents, where the need for magically disconnected presentations is almost absolute. More trout have been educated by catch-and-release. On waters where a direct delivery might have worked years ago, despite putting the leader over the fish before the fly got to it, the same cast today would cause a sophisticated trout to frown. Positive- and negative-curve casts can be used to hook a fly around at the end of the leader, delivering the fly to the fish first, even in the absence of obstacles.

THE POSITIVE-CURVE CAST

The positive-curve cast is delivered with the rod tilted toward the water. The leader turns in at the end of the cast; a positive curve hooks to the left for the right-handed caster, to the right for a left-handed caster.

The positive-curve cast is started with normal fore- and backcasts, but with the rod held parallel to the water. The line tours back and forth at about belt height. The line loops unfurl horizontal to the stream surface rather than high in the air and vertical to it. This is a cast that can easily wait until you are able to execute the basic cast with precision. It will be far easier to learn after you have gained loop control.

When the cast has been measured and the line extended to the right length in the air, you are ready for the delivery stroke. All that goes before it is normal casting with the rod tipped over.

The final delivery stroke is overpowered. The leader responds by accepting the extra energy of the line and kicking around beyond straight. If you were casting normally, with the loop vertical, the fly would kick downward and float to the surface ahead of the leader. With the rod canted, the leader boots the fly around in an arc, in toward an imaginary line drawn on the water straight upstream from the casting position. The result is a positive-curve cast.

The problem in calculating the final landing place of the fly rests in determining how much extra power in the cast results in how much hook in the leader. Too little power and the leader

The positive curve cast hooks left for the right-handed caster, and would hook right for the left-handed angler.

straightens without hooking at all. Too much power and the leader hooks too far around, delivering the fly alongside the following line.

The positive-curve cast can be elusive. It takes lots of practice. Even to the practiced, it doesn't fall the way you want it every time. But it can be mastered, and mastering it will help you jump quite a few fish that you otherwise might not have a chance to barb at all.

THE NEGATIVE-CURVE CAST

The negative-curve cast starts with the rod tilted in the same manner as the positive-curve cast, but depends on the loop landing on the water while still open, rather than after it has kicked around. A right-handed caster delivering a negative curve places the fly to the right of the line of the cast; a left-hander places the fly to the left of the line of the cast.

The negative-curve cast is more difficult to master than the positive curve. It is started in the same way, with the rod canted outward, the casting loops roving back and forth at belt line or just above it. When the cast is measured and the loop under control, it is time for the delivery stroke.

The delivery is made with an underpowered forecast. The goal is to lob the line out and have it land before the loop finishes unfurling. The calculations that you must make are a combination of the forward movement of the line and the rate at which the line descends toward the water. The line must land when the fly is where you want it and the loop is bent the way you want it.

A friend of mine was a helicopter pilot in Viet Nam. He told me that when coming into a landing zone under fire, he always combined a turn with his descent. Machine gunners were then forced to calculate lead in three directions: below him, in front of him, and in the direction of the turn. It cut their chances of hitting him in half, which was sufficient because he made it home to tell me about it.

The problem with the negative-curve cast is not so dramatic, but contains the same elements that you have to calculate, and they cut the chances for a good delivery about in half, too. Figuring out how much to underpower a cast so it lands when it's in the right place and the loop is formed the way you want it is a tough routine that seldom becomes routine at all. And like a bullet, once you've pulled the trigger on the cast, all you can do is watch to see if you've hit or missed. Too much power and the loop straightens out, or even embarrasses you by hooking into a

The negative curve cast falls to the right for the right-handed caster, and would fall left for the left-handed caster.

positive curve. Too little power and the line piles into the water several feet short of where you want it. Since the objective of the negative curve is usually to get a fly floating downstream to a fish rising above you, having the loop land too soon usually means it has landed on the head of the fish. You are then shot down. If the cast is made in an attempt to get the fly above an obstacle, a short round places the fly on top of the obstacle. It happens to me a lot.

The positive curve is easier to use than the negative curve. But both should be practiced, and learned to whatever degree seems possible short of lots of frustration. They'll take you a trout now and then that you would otherwise not have taken.

Keep both of the curve casts short, within twenty-five feet, and you'll get a higher percentage of good behavior out of them.

6

The Steeple Cast

The purpose of the steeple cast is to clear objects that stand tall enough behind you to block a normal backcast. If the objects are trees that crowd your heels and tower to the sky, the steeple cast won't do it for you. Save yourself the agony and use the roll cast instead. If the objects are shrubs, small trees, or a steep bank, and they give you room to operate your rod through a full casting motion, the steeple cast can give you a better presentation than the roll cast.

Many times brush and tall grass behind you seem to be tall enough to present an obstacle, but actually are not a problem at all if you just alter your cast a bit. Perhaps these short obstacles are the ones to climb over first.

TILTING THE CASTING PLANE

In the chapter on the basic cast, I pointed out that the cast operates correctly when the line straightens parallel to the ground in both forecast and backcast. If the forecast makes anything other than a straight line coming off the backcast, you will get tailing loops. But as long as you keep the casting plane straight, you can tilt it any way you please.

The easiest way to clear low objects in your backcast area is to tilt the casting plane down in front, which raises it up in back.

Begin with the basic cast, extending line until it reaches the point where the backcast must climb in order to clear an object. Now simply aim your forecast at a point just above the water. When the line straightens, draw the backcast up so that it is thrown over your shoulder in the same plane taken by the forecast. The result will be a level casting plane with a high backcast.

You can think of this in terms of the casting arc. The normal cast operates with a power stroke that throws the line straight back. When you tip the power stroke forward, the casting plane tilts, too, and the line will rise above the rod tip on the backcast rather than shooting straight behind it. The more tilt to the power stroke, and therefore to the casting plane, the higher the backcast will climb.

There are obvious limits to this procedure. You can only alter the plane until the line galumphs into the water on the forecast.

By tipping the power arc forward, you can often tilt the casting plane far enough to clear obstacles behind you without resorting to the roll cast or steeple cast.

Different casting positions allow different degrees of tilt. If you are wading deep, your forecast is already close to the water, and it's impossible to tilt it much. If you are standing on the bank, you can lower your forecast much more, and get a much higher back-cast. If the bank is a high one, you might be able to cast nearly straight up and down.

Because the tilt is limited by the distance you stand above the water, and because you can't stand very far above the water without exposing yourself to the trout, the cast with a tilted plane is limited to relatively short situations. A thirty-foot cast, when you are wading and clearing obstacles on the bank, would be a good one. A forty-five-to fifty-foot tilted cast is about the maximum even when you stand on a bank above the water.

THE STEEPLE CAST

The true steeple cast takes the line out of the level casting plane. The result is a cast that often gives you trouble, in the form of a tailing loop, even if you do it right. But it can get your backcast above very tall obstacles, and your fly to the water in places you could not fish otherwise.

The steeple cast starts with a backcast power stroke that tosses the line almost straight up over your shoulder. Most of the time it helps to turn and reverse the rod hand so that the wrist tosses the backcast upward almost as if it were a forecast. The power arc should be short and crisp, almost a flip to get the line towering up there above and slightly behind you.

The first forecast is usually the delivery stroke; you don't want to do a lot of extra backcasting with the steeple cast. The forecast begins with the line high overhead. Instead of powering the line straight down out of the backcast, keeping the casting plane level, make a normal forecast that drives the rod tip, and there-fore the line, at where you want the fly to land straight out in front of you. This is where the problems occur, and they are not your fault.

When the forecast and backcast are not on the same plane, the line has to go in two directions at once, both down and forward, and the result is a tailing loop. The tail end of the line scoops down below the part nearer the rod. The fly and leader undercut

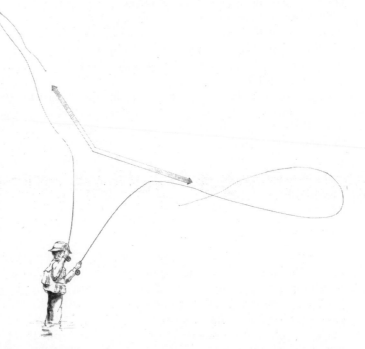

The back- and forecast of the steeple cast are not in the same plane. This often causes tailing loops even when you execute the cast correctly. They can be avoided to a certain extent by holding your casting arm as high as you can, and casting with an open, rolling loop.

the line. They often tangle when they cross each other, which they must do out toward the end of the cast, just before the leader turns over and the fly lands on the water.

On a short cast you can tame this problem by holding your rod high and throwing a wide loop on the forecast, accomplished by moving the rod tip through a long arc. This throws the upper part of the loop over the lower part as it unfurls. On a cast longer than about thirty feet you will have to toss the backcast into its steeple, make your normal forecast, and live with an occasional tangled tailing loop. The longer the attempted cast, the more likely you are to get tangled.

LOOKING FOR GAPS IN THE BACKCAST AREA

A final solution to a blocked backcast area is to turn around and look for holes in it. Often there are gaps between trees or in the brush that you can sneak a backcast into. If there are, you can position yourself to watch your backcast instead of your forecast, turning to the front only to aim the final presentation stroke.

You will be served well by whatever you have learned in terms of loop control, ability to tilt the plane of the cast, and ease of changing direction of the cast. Sometimes a tight loop helps you get away with a backcast into a narrow niche. You might have to tilt the plane of the backcast up to hit a high opening, or possibly down to hit a low one. If the opening is not in a straight line with your target, then you can extend your line in one direction, and make a change of direction on the final delivery stroke, placing the fly to the right or the left as you wish.

Watching the backcast area becomes almost an instinct, especially for those who fish small- to medium-sized streams. Huckleberry and alder are problems on almost every cast. The experienced angler quickly sizes up the necessary backcast, seemingly without even looking. He chooses between the steeple cast or the tilted plane without thinking about it. The final cast is often a combination of the two, with some elements of loop control and change of direction mixed in.

Control over all aspects of the cast is gained through *practice* first and *experience* second. One doesn't add up to much without the other. The more control you learn over all the aspects of casting, the more places you will be able to fish your flies to the surprise of the trout.

7

Single and Double Hauls

I fished the Deschutes River once with Steve Penner. As we drifted between trout runs in Steve's McKenzie boat, we came across a fellow wading deep and casting long. He was reaching out for summer steelhead, using the classic double-haul technique, driving his rod-arm shoulder into each stroke and ending each cast with his line hand flung far behind him. His girlfriend stood on the bank; every time he shot his final delivery he looked around to see if she had noticed.

His double haul was vigorous, almost violent, but it was laid atop a basic casting stroke that wasn't well designed. His loops were erratic; most of his casts, even when double-hauled, piled in at fifty feet. On one cast he contrived a tangle. On a couple of casts, during our float past him in the boat with its tipped-up ends, the line shot out sixty feet and landed straight.

Those casts were his goal. They were the only ones he wanted. The rest of them were preparation, and from the looks of the way he worked at each cast, he must have tired out soon.

If that fisherman would have ironed out his basic casting

stroke, he could have cast his sixty feet without any haul at all. And that's far enough to catch most trout, and most summer steelhead, too. Had he laid the double haul over the top of a smooth casting stroke, he could have punched out sixty-five to seventy feet of line on every cast, with little effort. Even the simpler single haul could have accomplished that.

Casting within control should always be your first goal. The alternative is a poor presentation, which rarely fools a trout whether the fly is a dry, wet, nymph or streamer. Striving for distance beyond your abilities tires you out quickly. Practice sessions end without the progress they could have provided. Fishing days end in frustration, and too often end fishless. Casting must become secondary to fishing. Your practice, on the stream and off, should slowly enable you to remove your concentration from casting to the things that surround you when you are fishing.

Distance casting almost always gets in the way of catching fish, for the beginning fly fisherman, because it constantly cuts into control. I went through it and you will, too: We strive to impress whoever is around; if nobody else is around we strive to impress ourselves.

This chapter on the single and double hauls is about how to cast long. But it begins with a finger-wagging admonition not to apply these techniques before you have mastered the basic casting stroke.

THE SINGLE HAUL

The purpose of the single haul is to boost your line speed a bit. This can do one of two things for you. First, it can give you five to fifteen feet of extra shoot on the delivery stroke. Second, and perhaps more useful in trout fishing situations, it can make your casts at normal distances just a bit easier, rendering casting throughout the day slightly less tiring. The single haul is effective for casts out to about sixty feet.

Preparation for the single haul is exactly the same as for the basic casting stroke. The rod hand holds the cork grip, with the thumb aligned down its back. The line hand holds the line, generally in two or three loose coils that fall to the water, or to the lawn in a practice session.

The backcast is made the same way that you would make it for the basic stroke. The single haul is designed to add distance to your cast; you should strive for a tight loop on the backcast because it cuts less air and is in itself an element of a long cast. You will achieve more distance by practicing until you can cast a tighter loop than you will achieve by trying to add a single haul to a cast with an open loop.

As the line straightens out behind you on the backcast, and the rod drifts back to the 45-degree position, allow your line hand to drift up close to the reel. When the forecast begins, the rod should be back, the line should be straight in the air, and your two hands should be within about a foot of each other. If you have trouble thinking about it in any other way, concentrate on putting your line hand right in front of your chin.

The loading movement of the rod, driving the butt forward a foot or so, serves to straighten any slack out of the line, and brings it tight against your line hand. This is the essential connection in the single haul. If there is any slack in the line when you make your line-hand movement, it will merely serve to draw that slack out in a hurry. It won't do a thing for your cast.

The single-haul movement is executed by drawing the line hand down swiftly at the same time that you put the power stroke into the rod. Timing is critical, but easy to master. After a practice session, your hands will have figured out the timing without bothering you with the details. In fact, that's the way it's got to be, because the single haul must be a swift movement, and you want to practice it until you can do it without taking time to think about it. The line is released for the shoot exactly at the end of the downward draw, which is the end of the power stroke.

The single haul does two things to the cast: it draws the rod into a deeper bend, and it gives the line a boost in speed. Both of these add distance to your forward cast. The deep bend in the rod makes it a more tightly wound spring. When it releases, it does so with more force. The faster line speed does the same thing speed does to a thrown stone: the faster it starts, the farther away it lands.

The single haul-movement can vary from a short downward flick of your wrist to a long, sweeping draw of the line hand until it is extended out behind you. The short quick movement is the

At the beginning of the single haul, the line hand is held near the reel. During the power stroke it is drawn sharply down, helping to accelerate the line.

one many fly fishermen use constantly and subconsciously, as part of the normal cast. Some use it even on a short cast. I do.

If I am caught kneeling in a tight situation on a small, brushy stream, I sometimes use a casting stroke that is not much more than simultaneous twitches of both wrists. The one pops the rod through a short casting arc, the other loads it a bit more and speeds the line. This method is good enough for casts up to about twenty-five feet, and it gets the line out there with so little movement that the fish are less likely to detect my presence.

The most common line-hand movement is a downward draw of a foot or two. This is a comfortable amount of movement, and it adds considerable force to a cast. It is common for an experienced trout fisherman to add a bit of single haul to almost every cast made, even at medium range. A forty- to fifty-foot cast with a touch of haul requires little effort from the rod hand, wrist, and arm. At the end of the day they will still be strong, and your wrist will not be sore.

The full sweep of a single haul, drawing the line hand down and back as far as you can from the rod hand, is the maximum use of the single haul. It is such a long movement that it becomes part of both the loading and power strokes of the rod. The draw begins as soon as the rod moves forward. It accelerates into a swift movement, almost jerking the line, when the rod arcs over in the power stroke.

This full movement is usually excessive unless it is combined with a haul movement on the backcast as well as the forecast. Then it becomes the double haul, which is designed to give you even more distance.

THE DOUBLE HAUL

The double haul is a simple extension of the single haul, and shouldn't be used until the easier technique is mastered. It requires some extra movements; if the basic stroke and then the single haul cannot be executed smoothly, then it's awfully easy to get tangled up trying to perform the double haul.

The double haul is built for distances beyond sixty feet. Its usefulness in trout stream situations is obviously limited to big water. My first bit of advice about its use would be to try to wade into a better casting position so you don't have to use it at all. But everybody knows that the biggest trout are always on the far side of the pool. Sometimes it's desirable to reach out there; sometimes it's fun. One thing is certain: those who can cast across the pool with comfort and ease are going to be able to catch some trout that other folks can't reach.

The double haul has little place when fishing with tackle suited to delicate presentations. It is usually used with medium or big rods, $8\frac{1}{2}$ feet long and longer, for 6-weight lines and heavier. If you strive for distance, it's important to do it with equipment designed for it. It is just as important to be sure that the line is matched to the rod, and that the leader suits the line at its butt and the fly at its tippet. The double haul will only magnify kinks in casting that are caused by mismatched tackle.

The double haul is the same as the single haul with the addition of a line-hand movement on the backcast. Let's look at it.

Begin with a basic casting stroke, fore- and backcasting to get about forty feet of line in the air. If you are using a weight-forward line, then the haul should begin when you've got the heavy line extended just a foot or two beyond the rod tip. With a double-taper line you want only the length of line in the air that the rod will carry without strain. The purpose of the double haul is to allow you to shoot more line, not to carry more line in the air. Each rod-and-line combination has a length of line at which it feels sweet; beyond that it's overloaded. Practice with your outfit until you learn how much line it likes to carry, then learn to shoot line beyond that length.

The double haul begins on the backcast. Start the movement with the line straightened in the air in front of you, the rod in the 45-degree position, and your line hand up near your rod hand, or in front of your chin, as it was on the single haul.

Hold the line hand in position while you draw the rod back in the loading stroke. As the rod moves back, the fixed-line hand will help take any slack out of the line, and will help load the rod against a tight line.

The line-hand movement for the double haul is a crisp downward draw made at the same time that the rod is forced into the backcast power stroke. This does the same thing the line hand movement does on the single haul: it loads the rod into a deeper

The double haul (clockwise from upper left) begins with a sharp downward draw of the line hand during the power movement of the back stroke. The line hand is allowed to drift back up to the reel, until it is in position next to it for the forward power stroke. When that stroke is made, the line hand draws down exactly as it did on the single haul. When the forward power stroke has been made, the line is released for the final shoot.

bend, and accelerates the line to a higher speed. It is important to stop the rod at the end of the power stroke, just as you would with a normal casting stroke without the haul involved. Again, a tight loop is essential to a long cast.

As the line straightens on the backcast, let the line hand drift back up to the proper position, near the reel or in front of your chin, for the forecast. This is easy to do, but it is the most difficult part of the double haul because you've got to concentrate on getting your hand up there where it needs to be.

This line-hand drift must be drawn up by the tug of the line as it straightens behind you. If you force it up too soon, you merely push slack into the line—it's like trying to push up a balloon with a string. If you bring the hand up too late, after the line has straightened behind you, there will be no line movement left to take out the slack you introduce. When you bring the rod forward to load and then power it, the slack will absorb all your effort and the line will come hooping over your head, or collapse all around you. As with all fly casting, timing is very important in the double haul.

The second movement in the double haul is a repetition of the single haul on the forecast. The line hand holds still for the loading of the rod on the forward stroke, then draws down swiftly as the power stroke is made.

If the first double haul leads into the delivery stroke, then the line is released for the shoot at the completion of the downward draw. If the first double haul is used to extend the line to the proper casting distance, and to build line speed, then the backcast and forecast movements are repeated, and the line is released for the shoot at the end of the second double haul. This sequence of one fore- and backcast to extend line, and a second to shoot it, is the most common double-haul sequence.

A third double haul will add nothing of speed and power to your cast if the first two are executed correctly. The only reason to perform a third full-casting movement is to straighten out an error introduced earlier. This is common, especially at first, and should not be sniffed at. Often while fishing I miss my timing on the fore- or backcast, and have to do it once again to get the line extended the right length and straight in the air. When a stroke is scrambled, it is usually in the timing of the line-hand drift into the high position for the downward sweep.

The most common use of the double haul is a couple of short draws, a foot or two long, to help load the rod and accelerate the line on both forecast and backcast. This gentle and graceful movement can make a fifty-five- to sixty-five-foot cast a lot easier, and less tiring.

The full draw of the double haul is seldom used unless you strive for casts from seventy to 100 feet. When the full draw is used, it is common to let the rod drift far back on the backcast, and far forward on the forecast. When the rod is allowed to drift, it extends the distance it can travel on the loading stroke. If your rod arm is straight in front of you or behind you, and the rod is extended too, you can draw the tip several feet in the loading movement. This puts a far deeper bend into the rod, and accelerates the line to a higher speed before the power stroke begins. But recall that the power stroke must travel in the same short arc as it does on any cast, or you merely toss it into an open loop, which won't give you any distance no matter how hard you throw it.

The double haul should only be used to cast distance you can handle with a degree of grace. Practice it, and let it become part of your normal casting when you are casting long for you—that might be forty-five or fifty feet. It is the extension of grace, not the extension of uncontrolled line, that will in time make you a better distance caster.

8

Mending and Tending Line

Moving water gives you lots of reasons to tend to your line once the cast is complete and the line is on the surface. With proper line control you can extend the free float of a dry fly, the deep drift of a nymph, or the coaxing swing of a wet fly or streamer. You can use line control to achieve more depth with a nymph, more speed or less in your retrieve of a streamer or wet. Line control also keeps you in position to set the hook when a trout strikes a fly fished upstream.

There are three elemental ways to control line: drawing it in, mending it upstream or down, and feeding it out. Once these three are mastered, there is an infinity of combinations of them that will allow you to cause your fly to dance like a puppet in almost any way you want it.

There are some tackle factors that affect line control. You can mend a floating line best, though you can adjust the lie of a sinking line in the instant after it lands, before it sinks. A double-taper line is easier to tend unless the cast is shorter than the heavy portion of a weight-forward taper. The lighter running line of a weight-forward won't lift the heavier casting line off the water. Control of the line on the water is one of the major reasons many experienced trout fishermen still use the old double-taper line most of the time. It is true for me.

You can mend the floating portion of a combination floating/ sinking line. It is easiest to control a 10-foot wet-tip, harder to control a 20-foot wet-belly, difficult to do much with a 30-foot wet-head. In order to mend effectively, the floating part of the line must be clean and dressed, so that it rides high in the surface film. This is true for a full-floating line as well: keep it clean and dressed, and you enhance both casting comfort and line control.

The longer the rod, the more control you have over the line on the water. Consider the rod a lever: the longer the lever, the more you can pry at the line. You can lift a long rod high to loft the afterportion of the line above a current that conflicts with the forward portion, out where the fly floats or tumbles along. Short rods subtract from line control; it is one reason behind the trend to take advantage of the efficiencies of graphite, and go to rods $8\frac{1}{2}$ to 9 feet long.

DRAWING LINE IN

The most common reason to draw line toward the rod is to keep pace with the float of a dry fly or nymph fished with an upstream cast. If you fail to keep up, you will not be in position to set the hook when a trout strikes the fly. If there is more slack on the water in front of you than you can remove by lifting the rod, then a hit will result in a miss. If you can only set the hook by driving the rod far back over your shoulder, to take out all of the slack, you will be in no position to play the fish once you've gotten the hook into it.

Drawing line is easy to accomplish, though at first you can expect to be awkward when casting straight up into a swift current. The hands do the job, and it takes both of them working in concert. The line hand draws the line in, pulling it over the rod-hand forefinger—that busy finger again. When the line hand is fully extended, and can draw in no more line, it can either let the line go or keep its grip and hold the line that's been drawn in as a coil for the next cast. Either way, the line hand comes back to the rod hand to get a new grip on the line. This should be a smooth but fast movement, to reduce the amount of time the line hand is out of control of the line. As the movement is made, the rod-hand forefinger holds the line against the middle finger. If a fish hits at that moment, you are still in control and can set the hook.

When drawing line in ahead of the drift of a dry fly, you should remove all the slack you can without hindering the movement of the fly. Keep most of the slack out, but leave enough to give the fly its freedom. Keep the rod low. It should be held nearly level unless you are holding it high to keep the line above a conflicting current.

When keeping pace with the downstream drift of a nymph fished upstream, the most critical factor is determining a take. The more line you can keep off the water, the better you can tell when something odd happens to the line tip, or to your strike indicator. This calls for holding the rod high. With a high rod you've got to draw the line in precisely, not letting any slack form, but also not letting the lofted line tug at the leader and upset the natural tumble of the nymph. It is difficult to set the hook with a high rod. That is why, when you watch a nympher at work, he holds the line hand fairly close to the reel, and draws it down sharply whenever he lifts the rod at a suspected take. With the high rod there isn't much lift left, and this sharp drawing-in of line serves to set the hook.

Drawing line is an effective tactic to control the speed of the swing of a wet fly or streamer. Say you are casting across-stream, or across and down, in what is commonly called *frog water:* a run or pool with a slow current. This kind of water holds trout, sometimes uncommonly large ones. But the current isn't always strong enough to swing a fly, activate it, make it lifelike. You must quicken it. Do it by steadily drawing in just enough line to speed up the swing of the fly.

An obvious reason to draw line toward you is to accomplish the active retrieve of a nymph, wet fly, or streamer. You can do it with a slow hand-twist, gathering the line by rolling it over the thumb and then little finger of your line hand. For a faster retrieve, take in the line with short strips: draw four inches to a foot of line over the rod-hand forefinger, get a new grip with the line hand, do it again, and again and again. It's an effective wet fly

The upstream nymph fisherman holds his rod high for more control over the drift. In order to set the hook he must use a quick downward draw of the line hand. Dave Hughes

and streamer retrieve because it copies the way a lot of aquatic animals move. To mimic the way some baitfish swim, draw in the line with longer sweeps of the line hand. You can add some action to any of the retrieves by twitching the rod tip while drawing in the line. Sometimes that's just what the trout demand.

MENDING LINE

Mending line is what we think about when we think about tending line. Though it is only one way to do it, it is possibly the most important way. A mend is, at its simplest, simply an up- or downstream movement of the rod that lifts the line off the water, rolls it over in the desired direction, and sets it back down in the opposite curve from which it started.

Water moves the line in several wrong directions that mends can help correct. When casting across an even current, the thicker middle of the line catches more current and is pushed downstream faster than the finer tip and leader. The result is a downstream arc in the line, called a *downstream belly*, that takes the slack out of a cast and then drags the fly after the line. An *upstream belly* can form when you cast across a slow current into a faster one. Mends can eliminate both upstream and down-stream bellies.

A mend can be used to put slack back into the line to extend the drift of a dry fly. Usually this happens after the current has removed S-turns installed by a slack-line cast, and turned them into a downstream belly. An upstream mend keeps the line from drawing tight against the fly.

Mends can also be used to control the swing of a wet fly or streamer. A downstream mend will cause the line to catch the current and form a belly, speeding the fly swing. An upstream mend will eliminate a downstream belly and slow the swing. Constant mends of a cross-stream cast can let the fly drift down-stream as if it were dissattached from the line and leader. This is called the *greased-line* method; its applications were designed for salmon and steelhead fishing. The method was translated for trout fishing with wet flies by Sylvester Nemes, in *The Soft-Hackled Fly* (Chatham Press, 1975.)

The depth achieved by a nymph fished cross-stream can be controlled by mending the line. If the cast is made just upstream of straight across, and the line is not allowed to belly down-stream and tug against the fly, drawing it toward the surface, the nymph will sink a foot or two deeper. The upstream mend will also make the difference between a nymph that is pulled unnatu-rally by the line, and a nymph that drifts freely with the current. Trout notice such things. You should, too. Expert nymph fisher-men mend on almost every cast, usually the instant the line lands, and several times during the drift.

Executing a mend is easy, especially on a cast at reasonable trout-fishing range: thirty to forty feet. To make an upstream mend, first draw in whatever slack lies between the rod and the belly of line you want to remove. At the same time, align your rod with the line, pointing it at the belly and dropping the tip low to the water. Now simply roll the rod over in a long upstream arc. The line will follow, lifting off in a downstream belly, looping over, and landing in an upstream belly. When the current has pushed the line into a downstream belly again, repeat the proc-ess. Each mend should give you a few extra feet of free float.

The longer the line you have on the water, the more vigorous your mend must be. Lift the rod high and roll it over hard. With a

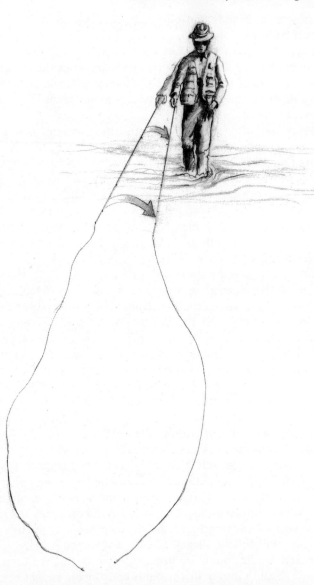

A mend is accomplished by lifting the rod and flipping it over in an arc. This lifts the line off the water, and tosses the belly in the opposite direction. The more vigorous the movement, and the higher the rod is lifted, the more line will be mended.

long rod and a well-dressed floating line, you can draw your elbow in just before the mend, then drive it out with the mend. The result is a corkscrew effect, a cross between a mend and a roll cast. The line will land on the upstream side with a couple of curves in it, rather than the even arc achieved by the straight mend. But the curves are slack, and getting slack into the line where you want it is what mending is all about.

The downstream mend is used less frequently, usually when crossing opposing currents with a dry fly, or trying to speed the swing of a wet fly or streamer. It is made with the same movements as the upstream mend. The rod is lowered and pointed down the line, and all the slack line is drawn out. Then the rod is rolled over to lift the line and loop it to the opposite side, forming a downstream belly that the opposing currents will slowly push out. Repeat as it is needed.

Often an effective mend is a mere flick of the wrist. This is usually true when fishing short, or when the belly you want to remove is slight and near the rod. A belly that forms out near the fly is difficult to remove with a mend, especially if the cast is over forty feet. In that case, either work with a shorter drift and more frequent casts, or wade into a position that gives you a better casting angle, one that won't result in a bellied line.

FEEDING LINE

Feeding line into a drift is too simple to spend much time talking about. But at times it helps take trout, and it is good to know when to do it, and how it's done.

Line fed through the guides can extend the drift of a dry fly when it is cast across stream, or downstream. These kinds of casts are normally made with slack in the line; by feeding more slack behind that gained by the cast, the drift can be extended several feet. Line can also be fed into the drift of a cross-stream nymph, to keep it drifting freely and to help it attain extra depth. Feeding line into the downstream swing of a wet fly or streamer is an effective method for slowing the fly, when the current gets it going too fast to estimate the way anything in nature might move.

To feed line into a drift, simply ease it out with the line hand, controlling the amount released and its speed with the forefinger of the rod hand. Let it go fast or slow, depending on how you want the line to affect the fly.

Another way to feed line out is to make the cast, then draw extra line off the reel, and immediately roll it out onto the water in front of the rod. This method is usually used to set up a wet-fly or streamer swing downstream farther than you could cast. For example, if you've waded as far as you dare, and there is still good water below you, cast across and toss slack onto the water. The line will continue to lie across the current, the way you want it, moving downstream in a piece while the slack feeds straight downstream from the rod. When the fly reaches the point where you want it to begin its swing, simply tighten on the line and it will swim across farther below you than you could have cast.

A final way to feed slack into a cast is to wobble the rod briskly while releasing the line behind the stripping guide. This is the same method used to get out the first few feet of line for a roll cast. The wobbled rod tip draws line through the guides and drops it to the water right in front of you, in tight S-turns. These turns feed out behind the moving line; it is an effective method to extend the drift of a dry fly cast downstream, or quartering down and across the current. It has the disadvantage of laying lots of slack on the water between you and the fly. When you get a strike you'll have to set vigorously. If you miss you are likely to blow the line over your head. It can get exciting.

AERIAL MENDS

After you have learned full control of the basic fly cast, it is possible to make the cast with a mend while the line is still in the air. The advantage is obvious: when fishing over currents that you know will immediately cause the line to belly, and the fly to drag, you can cause the fly to land with an opposite belly already installed. This gives you a few feet of free drift while the current pushes the arc out of the line and then arcs it again in the direction that will cause the drag.

Like all other casts, aerial mends should be practiced short first, preferably in conditions where you are not surrounded by difficulties. A lawn or lake is fine, but so is a broad riffle or run, which is the kind of water where the method is most useful.

To make an aerial mend, do the basic fore- and backcasts, and drive the rod into the delivery stroke. While the line still straightens in the air, push the rod over in the direction you want the mend to go. Then return the rod to the normal casting position. The push will cause a wave to form down the line. When the line lands, this wave will be a mend lying on the water.

The bigger and longer the push you give the line, the larger the mend when it falls. The sooner you give it as the line straightens out, the farther the mend will land from the rod. The later you give it, the closer the mend will be to the rod.

This is a rather esoteric technique, one you won't use often. Most of the time, the reach cast will do the same job, and it's easier. But the aerial mend is a good one to have in your mix of casting tricks. It will help you catch an occasional trout that lies where you can't otherwise get a good drift over it. The cast will certainly help you impress your friends, and that's a valid reason to learn a cast.

The goal of fly fishing, as I might have mentioned before, is control. Mending and tending line, on the water and in the air, backs up your casting skills and gives you more control over the drift or retrieve of your flies.

Creative line control, combined with creative casting, can help you make your flies look more like something a trout would want to eat.

9

Wading as Part
of the Cast

When you think about the whole problem of getting a fly in front
of a trout, casting covers only the last few feet of it. The cast is
the delivery stroke. Wading is what gets you into position to
make the cast one that works.

WADING FOR POSITION

When you approach either a rising trout, or a lie that looks
promising, the first thing to do is to assess the situation. Determine the holding position of the seen or suspected fish. You want
to know where the rise or the take begins, not where it ends. In
most water a trout drops downstream with its victim, and the
take is below the point where the insect was spotted by the trout.
Then the rise form itself – the circle that you see on the water –
drifts down with the current. Cast to the rise rings, and you
might place your fly two to ten feet below the trout, which has by
then returned to its original lie.

After you have figured out where the trout holds, or might hold if the lie looks good but the trout is not visibly feeding, then you want to determine how the trout's food arrives to its position. Your goal is to present an artificial in the manner that a natural would arrive in front of the fish. If the fly is a perfect imitation, but moves in an unlikely way, the fish will not want it.

The water and its currents become the boss: they tell you how to position yourself and how to cast, whether the fly is a dry, a subsurface wet, a nymph, or a streamer. Assess the situation and see how you can use the currents to deliver your fly. Sometimes the water will require a downstream float or drift, sometimes upstream, sometimes straight across stream.

Once you have determined the lie of the fish, and the way you want to present your fly to it, then you can see the position you must take in order to make it happen. If that position is workable, then you should move into it without spooking the fish. If it is unworkable because the water is too deep or too fast or the position is impossible to reach without spooking the fish, then you'll have to take a second choice. The unfavorable choice might reduce your chances of taking the trout, but that is the nature of fishing: you select tackle, hone your casting, and move into positions that give you the highest chance you can get. But trout fishing hinges on chance or you wouldn't be doing it in the first place.

You must move carefully into the selected position. You can't thrash out to the most favorable spot and expect to have much chance left of taking the fish. You've got to wade slowly enough to prevent wading waves from sweeping over the fish. This is easy in riffles and fast runs, but takes patience and a slow step in gentle runs, on flats, and when wading into pools.

You've got to move without scraping and clattering. A wading staff that bounces along behind you will scatter the trout ahead of you. If the bottom is unstable you've got to place your feet carefully to avoid knocking rocks together. Low-frequency sound travels well underwater. Scrapings and bangings that you never knew you made might cause the trout to duck for cover. If you carelessly approach a lie where you cannot see fish working, then you might fish it and not take anything, and consider it bad water when in truth it was good water until you arrived.

Wading into position calls for keeping your rod, your body, and your shadow out of sight of the fish. Keep the rod tip low; if the water is clear, keep the rod pointed behind you. As an extension of this, if the fish are so near and the water so clear that they might see the rod waving overhead on the cast, then tilt the casting plane so the rod is parallel to the water. The line will follow the plane of the rod; you can keep everything out of sight until the delivery stroke. If you have planned your position correctly, and made your cast right, the delivery should show the trout the fly first, as if it arrived there to its own surprise.

If you move into position on visibly feeding trout, and they are slightly disturbed by your presence, it is possible at times to be patient and let them return to a steady feeding rhythm. Trout are not long on recall. It's possible for them to forget you are around, especially if they are intent on whatever is hatching. But you've got to keep any wading waves down, and your rod and yourself out of sight, or you will merely put them down when you start fishing after they have started feeding again.

When you've waded carefully into the best casting position, you should be able to make your fly land as if to its own surprise, and the surprise of the trout. Katey Jones Hughes

WADING SAFELY

I covered wading equipment in the chapter on gearing up for trout fishing. Safe wading begins with the right gear: felt soles on clean bottoms, studs or cleats for algae-covered rocks. Your wading staff should be handy, tied to you, and not constantly tripping you up.

Wading safety is based largely on common sense. You should never wade fast over uneven bottoms. If you can't see the bottom, never move faster than your forward foot can feel out its options. Get it planted before you take the weight off the rear foot. If your trailing foot is not secure, and the forward foot finds itself groping, you're going down between them.

When fighting a current, always stop your wading short of depths that threaten to sweep you off your feet. This can be surprisingly shallow in strong rivers. Knee-deep in a swift tailout might be as far as you dare go. In some currents you can go in to your wader tops and not be in any danger.

When the current is pushy, lean on your staff in the *upstream* direction. That way you lean into the current rather than with it. If a foot or the staff should slip, the current catches you instead of toppling you. If you must wade with your staff downstream, then wade more slowly and keep two of your three legs – the staff and a foot or else both feet – planted at all times.

If you get into a position from which there is no extrication, don't panic. You might be in danger of getting wet and cold, but not much more. Keep your head attached, wade down with the current, and try to keep your feet in position to bounce on the bottom now and then, to kick you up. Navigate back toward shore at an angle, as you can.

If you get into a place where you can't reach bottom, then bring your feet up and float with them going downstream ahead of you. Your biggest danger is banging your head on a rock, and losing control. Keep your head up, and backpaddle with your hands to keep your feet in front, as shock absorbers. It has been said that wearing a wader belt cinched around your waist or chest will trap air, forcing your feet up and your head down. In the first place, when you are wading, that air will be forced out anyway; it's unlikely you will lose your footing with much air in your waders. In the second place, if there is air in them, it will float

your feet up, but it won't force your head down. You'll be glad
it's there.

If you get into a place where you are tugged under, then let
yourself go down until you can reach bottom with your feet. Kick
up toward the surface where you can get a gulp of air. If necessary, bounce along, kicking up to get air when you can, until you
reach shallower water.

Struggling to get your waders off in a bad situation will do no
good, especially if they are the stocking-foot kind, and your wading shoes are laced. Waders have essentially neutral buoyancy;
they might hinder your movements, but they won't pull you
down. Leave them on and save your energy to get to shore.

Neoprene waders are in themselves a form of life preserver.
They are thick, and full of trapped pockets of air. Fall in and they
will buoy you right back up. If you get into trouble in rapids, they
will also protect your legs and body from bangs and abrasions.
Whenever I float rivers like the Deschutes, especially in one of
my small boats that are marginal for the heavy rapids that are
sprinkled along the river, I wear neoprenes, adding a life jacket
when I approach a Class III or Class IV rapid. The sense of
security the neoprenes give is amazing. They let me get closer to
the edge, which is what makes river running more fun, which is
not what this book is about.

Neoprene waders are the ultimate safety device for the wading
angler. If you are at all timid about wading, then get a set. If you
will be wading dangerous or cold water, then use them. I mentioned that they tend to float you up a bit, and keep you from
wading quite so deep as you could without them. That in itself is
a safety feature: they keep you from wading where you shouldn't.

10

A Trout in the Hand

I have stated that the goal of fly fishing is control. The ultimate end of control is a trout held in your hand, or, if the trout is large, held in both hands. Everything that you do in selecting your casting position and wading to it – choosing the proper fly pattern and the presentation that makes it look like natural food, then executing the cast that brings the fly to the fish – leads to the moment when the trout takes the fly. From that instant, three things come into play before the fish can be brought to your hand. They are *setting the hook, playing the fish,* and *landing it.*

SETTING THE HOOK

Setting the hook to a visible take is easiest of all. You see it happen; you raise your rod to take any slack out of the line and to bring the hook home. The visible take is usually a splash to a dry fly. As a general rule, the quicker you set the hook, the more likely you are to get the hook set. But there is an essential exception.

The exception comes with the largest trout, which are the ones you most want to catch. A small trout normally takes a fly in a rush, and turns down with a flip and the fly already lodged inside its mouth. But big ones often take without the same haste. They come slowly, as if conserving energy, and turn down with dignity. A quick strike will often pull the fly away from them. When this happens, they will seldom come to the fly again.

It is not easy to tell the difference between a small trout and a big one by the take unless you can see the fish itself as it rises to the fly, or you can judge by the volume of water displaced that it is no ordinary trout. Either way, it is difficult to adjust a normal hasty hook set to a slow and deliberate one in reaction to the occasional and sudden sighting of a big one. If you have normal emotions, it's impossible. The best way to solve it, so that you catch the usual run of trout and don't blow your line over your back taking the fly away from the big ones, is to practice a strike that is not rushed.

The hook set should not be a jab that hits the fish, but a lifting movement that brings the hook point into it. Hold onto the line with your line hand, or draw line in if there is lots of slack on the water. Raise the rod firmly until it comes against the weight of the fish. Put the rod against this weight according to the size of hook and tippet with which you are fishing. If it's a small hook, #16 or under, and a fragile tippet, 3-pound test or less, don't get pushy. Such small hooks have fine points, and are easy to set into the flesh of the fish anyway.

If the fly is a large one, #10 and up, and the tippet strong, 5-pound test and stouter, you can give the fish a jab if you like, but *after* you have drawn the line up tight against it. The tippet will stand it, and the coarser hook might require it. But the need will be lessened if your hook is sharp and debarbed. I know of few hook manufacturers putting out hooks that are sharp enough to fish right out of the box. At least those in #12 and larger can almost always use touching up. I use a diamond fingernail file at the tying vise, and sharpen a hook before I tie a fly on it. On the stream, I have a nipper tool with a hook hone on it, and use it often.

A hook that is debarbed penetrates better than one that must pass the barb through the flesh of the fish. You will lose trout that are played carelessly, with slack in the line, but it's not because of the debarbed hook; it's because of the carelessness. As long as tension is held against the trout while you play it, you will not lose it because of a debarbed hook.

Setting the hook to an invisible strike is more difficult than it is with a visible strike. Takes of this type usually come to nymphs fished upstream. The difficulty is due to delay. By the time news of the take is transferred up the line to you, things have already happened down below, and are about to be over. You've got to get the hook set the instant you think that a fish has intercepted the fly.

The set itself should be a strong upward thrust of the rod – if anything, faster than the reaction to the take of a dry fly. Because the line and leader under the water will absorb much of the force of the hook set, it should be executed with a lot more force. But temper this with what you know about the amount of line in the water to absorb shock, and the strength of your tippet to withstand whatever is left of it that reaches the fly.

Whatever you can do to speed up the indication of a take will increase the number of times you get the hook into the fish. That is why most successful nymph fishermen now employ bright strike indicators. These not only let them know about most of the subtle takes they otherwise would miss, but also let them know about solid takes a lot sooner.

Setting the hook with an indicator requires the same quick upward lift of the rod to get slack out of the line. You should make this movement any time the indicator acts in contrast to the current. If it darts upstream, that is pretty obvious. More often, the indicator will hesitate. Sometimes the hesitation is almost imperceptible. I fished the San Juan River once with New Mexico Trout's Bob Cox and Farmington guide and fly shop owner Chuck Rizzuto. The water was cloudy, the trout were taking nymphs deep, but stopped the flies so subtly, and rejected them so swiftly, that I was rarely able to detect it.

Chuck and Bob would watch my indicator; every few minutes one would shout, "There!" But I would see nothing indicating a take, and my strike in reaction to their shout was usually too late. I took a few fish, and they were among the brightest and strongest I have caught. But both Bob and Chuck brought three times as many fish to the boat as I did. It takes a lot of nymph and indicator fishing to get the hang of spotting a take, and setting the hook. Expect to be frustrated at first.

It should be simple to set the hook to a strike that you feel. But it has its hidden complications. This kind of strike usually comes to a wet fly fished down and across the stream, to a nymph washed down through a riffle or run, or to a streamer fished on the swing.

The strike to a nymph or streamer is usually strong, and the fish either sets the hook or doesn't. Your job is to raise the rod at the report of the strike, and to begin playing the fish at once. It's simple. The complications arise in wet-fly fishing.

Trout often gently intercept wet flies fished on a slow swing. When they do, what you feel is not a rap, but an increasing tension on the line, as if it slowly gets heavier. The tendency with this discovery is to yank on the rod, to get the hook home before the fish lets go. This sort of hook set generally pulls the hook upstream and away from the fish. The proper hook set does nothing, and allows the tension to grow against the line until the fish either hooks itself or does not. It's not much more than a 50–50 proposition; it can be a frustrating game. It takes a lot of discipline to allow events to take their own course.

If trout take wet flies with a rap, then the proper reaction is to raise the rod. But when they take with a subtle increase of tension on the line, letting them set the hook themselves becomes an added challenge in the fishing. If you fish wet flies long enough, then this moment of increasing tension becomes the one you wait for most anxiously. It is hard to describe, but it brings to trout fishing that same suspense that summer steelhead anglers enjoy as they mark the take of a great fish, then discipline themselves to wait while the fish takes the fly down before seating the hook firmly into the corner of its jaw.

PLAYING THE FISH

The goal is control, and the only way to keep a fish under control is to keep the line tight between the rod tip and the trout's cavortings. Slack line gives the hook a chance to work out. It also gives the trout the chance to go where it wants, which is often to the nearest cover, where it can break you off.

Setting the hook brings the point of the hook into the fish. It also takes the slack out of the line. From that moment until the fish is in reach you must strive to keep the fish tugging directly against the rod tip.

Line is controlled after the cast, while the fly is still on the water coaxing the fish, by a combination of the line hand and the rod-hand forefinger working together. After a fish hits, this control is even more critical. The rod-hand finger becomes the drag; the line hand feeds line out or draws line in over it, depending on the direction of travel of the fish. If the fish is not large enough to make a strong run, thereby drawing out all of the slack between the stripping guide and the reel, then you can play it by hand.

Playing a fish by hand can be awkward at first. But the same stripping movements that are used to make a retrieve also serve to defeat a fish. Keep the line under control with the rod-hand forefinger. Use it as a drag, to feed line into runs, to take it in when you can. Each time the line hand has drawn in enough line so that it is fully extended, clamp down with the rod-hand forefinger while you let the line hand go to get a new grip on the line, near the reel.

It takes a little judgment to decide whether to play a fish by hand or on the reel. If a fish does not take all the slack out itself, then in order to get it on the reel you've got to hold the rod with the line hand and reel in with the rod hand. If your reel is reversed, then you've got to keep the rod hand's grip on the rod, and reel with the line hand. Either way, you must either let go of the slack line, or contrive a way to control it with the rod-hand forefinger while you reel. It's difficult. It's a good way to lose a fish. It should be done only if the trout holds against the rod tip with enough force so that the line remains tight. The instant the fish moves your way, and slack develops, stop reeling and gather in line by hand again.

Playing a fish off the reel is easier because you don't have to deal with line that coils around your feet, and you don't have to use your fingers for drag. Once a fish is taking line directly from the reel, then lots of your problems are solved. In its essence, all you do from then until the fish is within reach is reel when the fish moves your way, or when you can move it your way, and let the reel spin when the fish runs.

If you are playing a fish off the reel and it runs toward you faster than you can gather line by reeling, then stop, and strip line by hand until you've caught up with it. It is common for experienced anglers to deal with the resulting slack by allowing, even encouraging, the trout to make another run to get it back onto the reel again. But you can also reel up slack while the fish hangs against the current after its run, keeping the line tight by pressing it against the rod grip.

Whether you are playing a trout by hand or on the reel, the rod position should be high enough to put pressure on the fish, and to absorb the shock of any runs or sudden moves the fish might make. The higher the rod, the more of a shock absorber it becomes. A 30-to-45-degree angle is about right if the fish is far from the rod. This puts more butt strength against the fish, but depends on the line in the water to act as a shock absorber. The closer the fish comes to the rod, the higher the rod should be held. When the fight is in its finishing stages, the rod should be held nearly vertical to absorb any sudden lunges while the line is short.

The fish should be played until its vigor is diminished to the point where you can corral it. With a small fish, this might be while it's still flapping and splashing around. With a large trout, you might want to wait until it begins to wobble, turning toward its side. But if you intend to release the fish, you should get it in before it is completely exhausted. If there is a simple rule, it is that a fish is ready for landing when you can force its head up to the surface and hold it there. How soon that moment will arrive depends on the size of the fish and the stoutness of your gear. Make it happen as soon as you can, for the sake of the fish. The sooner you land it and release it, the higher its chance for survival.

LANDING TROUT

Once a fish is near enough to reach, then it's time to hold it in your hand. If you seriously want to hold it there, though, make sure that most of its energy has been wicked off. A green fish is almost impossible to subdue. If the fish is still thrashing and attempting to make runs, then let it make another before trying to bring it in. Let it fight the rod a while longer, until you can hold its head up.

The easiest way to land a fish is with a landing net. It can also be the gentlest, if you use a net with a cotton mesh. Nylon nets are harsh and abrasive; they can hurt fish that you want to release. The net should be hung about you in some manner that lets you extend it to the length of your arm. A lanyard and clip works fine; hook it to the back of your vest, which should have a D-ring at the nape of your neck. If it doesn't, a seamstress can easily sew one on. A net retriever, or a carpenter's retrieve, works better if the chain is long enough. Again, no matter how you hang your net, you should be able to extend your arm to land a fish with it.

When netting a fish, it is important that you be in control of the fish to the point that you can lift its head out of the water and hold it there, and lead it across the surface. When the fish has reached this point, and you have shortened the line and leader beyond the rod tip to a couple of feet more than the length of the rod, then extend the net and hold it half in and half out of the water. Lead the fish into the net by drawing the rod tip back. When the trout crosses the lip, lift the net, and you've got the fish.

Never stab the net at a trout, or try to submerge the net entirely and lift it under the fish. Either method will inspire the fish to a final burst of energy. If you stab at it, it will elude you, and you are liable to hit the leader and knock the fly away from the fish. If you try to swish the net under a fish, it will shoot forward, and the net will come up with the fish half in and half out. This makes for dramatic action, with the fish lifted high and flopping on the rim of the net. Once in a while you will be able to juggle it into the net; most of the time it will fall back into the water, often with the fly dislodged.

Once you've got the fish in the net, hold it gently but firmly in one hand, with a grip on the outside of the meshes. Work your other hand into the bowl of the net to the fish's jaw, remove the hook, then tilt the net to slip the trout gently back into the water. If the net gets slightly tangled, then untangle it so that the fish's gills are free. They are fragile, and easily injured by careless handling of the net.

Hand-landing a trout is more difficult than netting it, and requires a more subdued fish. Tire it out, get its head on the surface, then lead it to your hand. Your hand is not a net, but you

Whether you intend to land it by hand or with a net, you should always play a trout until you can lift its head to the surface and hold it there, or lead it to you. Dave Hughes

want to use it like one. Lead the fish over it, cradle the fish until its weight is balanced, then lift it out of the water. If the feel of your hand under it causes the trout to jet forward, then swing the trout around and bring it in again. If the fish is a small one, you can put your fingers around it to restrain it. But do so very gently; trout live in neutral buoyancy with water, and are very delicate internally. A squeeze can kill them.

A hand-landed fish can be lifted and held against your body in order to keep it from wiggling free while you remove the hook. If the hook is deep in the trout's throat, or lodged in hard bone, use your forceps to take it out.

If the fish squirms while you hold it, and it begins to slip, simply let it go, get out of the way, and it will drop into the water. If you intend to release it, obviously, it helps to hand-land it in water deep enough to protect it in such a fall. Move to the beach only with those trout you might want to kill. Once a trout has fallen to the water, use your rod to tire it again and bring it back to your hand.

If the fish is a big one, three pounds and up, use two hands to land it. Cradle its belly with one hand, kneel, tuck your rod under your armpit, then use the other hand to cradle it at the wrist of the tail. Lift it out gently.

I am a strong advocate of catch-and-release. About the only time I keep trout anymore is on waters with an abundance of them, when I want to keep a fish or two for a streamside fry. Never keep a fish from a stream that needs it. When the plan is to keep a fish, then it should be killed at once by a sharp rap on the head with a stone, knife handle, stick, or whatever else is handy. Make sure the job is complete; don't let a wounded fish flop around and suffer. Clean it immediately for the best flavor. Trout are too precious to kill without forethought, and far too valuable to waste if you do kill them.

If the fish is to be released, then get the hook out of it as soon as you can, and return it to the water. Often you can lead a fish to your feet, hold it with one hand, and twist the fly out with the other, all without ever removing the fish from the water. This is the best method for the fish.

A tired trout should not be given its freedom until it can keep itself upright and swim without wobbling. That is the highest reason for playing and landing the trout as quickly as you can, before it is worn out. If a fish is wobbly, hold it in a gentle current, with a grip on the wrist of its tail and a hand supporting its belly. Move it slowly back and forth into the current, to help get its gill rhythms back.

When a trout is ready, it will swim forcefully out of your hands.

Conclusion:
Creative Casting

In this book, I've covered tackle selection for trout fishing, and the several kinds of casts that make up the basis for trout-fishing techniques. Most of these casts are built on the basic fly cast.

The roll cast calls for the basic casting stroke with the line still on the water, using surface tension to load the rod. Slack-line casts are basic casts with the brakes put on, or with wobbles added, to serpentine the line. Reach casts are basic casts laid over to one side or the other, to extend the drift of a fly.

Positive- and negative-curve casts are basic casts with the loop tilted to one side, and either under- or overpowered. The steeple cast is the basic cast with the casting plane tilted down in front to elevate the backcast above brush in back. The single and double haul are line-hand movements added to the basic rod-hand casting stroke in order to add energy to the cast.

I mentioned at the beginning of the casting section of the book that fly casting was based on a few simple movements, and that once you had them down, *fly casting* became secondary and *fly fishing* moved into the foreground. I also mentioned a few creative casts in the book, for example, the roll cast pickup that lifts the fly from the water without disturbing the surface, and the aerial mend that delivers the line to the water with an upstream curve installed. These are just examples of the kinds of creative casting you can do once you've mastered the basic casting stroke.

Creative casting is at the heart of fly fishing. Once you've reached the point where the basic cast comes by instinct, and the rod and line begin telling you what they want done to them to accomplish a specific effect, then you can begin combining kinds of casts, or making up your own.

The first step in creating a cast is assessing the situation: what do you want to happen, and why? Size up the position of the sighted or suspected fish. Notice how the currents deliver food to the lie. Decide what you must make the line and leader do in order to get the fly to where you want it, floating or drifting or swimming the way you want it to. Then create the cast that makes it happen.

When you begin to approach trout fishing on this level, it takes on the nature of any creative endeavor: the satisfaction is in the accomplishment itself. The trout you catch will be affirmations.

Bibliography

Bergman, Ray. *Trout*. New York: Alfred A. Knopf, 1976.

Brooks, Joe. *Trout Fishing*. New York: Outdoor Life Books, 1972.

Haig-Brown, Roderick. *A Primer of Fly-Fishing*. Seattle: University of Washington Press, 1964.

Hughes, Dave. *Handbook of Hatches*. Harrisburg: Stackpole Books, 1987.

————. *Reading the Water*. Harrisburg: Stackpole Books, 1988.

Krieger, Mel. *The Essence of Flycasting*. San Francisco: Club Pacific, 1987.

McClane, A.J. *The Practical Fly Fisherman*. Englewood Cliffs, New Jersey: Prentice-Hall, 1953.

Morris, Skip. *The Custom Graphite Fly Rod*. New York: Nick Lyons Books, 1989.

Nemes, Sylvester. *The Soft-Hackled Fly*. Connecticut: Chatham Press, 1975.

Schwiebert, Ernest. *Trout*. New York: E.P. Dutton, 1978.

Scott, Jock. *Greased Line Fishing for Salmon (and Steelhead)*. Portland: Frank Amato Publications, 1982.

Swisher, Doug and Carl Richards. *Fly Fishing Strategy*. New York: Crown, 1975.

Index